Basic Catholicism

Deacon Douglas McManaman

Registered with the Canadian Intellectual Property
Office

ISBN: 978-0-9917996-5-7

Library and Archives Canada Cataloguing in
Publication

McManaman, Douglas

Dedication

To my wife Cecilia, with love

Table of Contents

You could say that this book began years ago as a response to my students' desire to learn something about the fundamental principles of Catholic theology, after studying 120 hours of philosophy. Sometimes students would, after graduating, return to ask me to write them something that would help them understand a particular point of Catholic doctrine; in fact, that is how Chapter 9 "An Exposition on the Trinity" came to be written—a former student wanted to be able to explain something about the Trinity to his Muslim friends. As my friend the late Monsignor Tom Wells once said to me, "It is amazing, after studying philosophy, how Catholic theology begins to make so much sense".

One day while visiting a friend of mine, Father Don Sanvido of the Diocese of Hamilton, I noticed an old tattered book on a table next to his cigarettes. The date of the imprimatur was 1938, so I began to read it. I was impressed with the simplicity, depth, and freshness of the writing, almost completely counterintuitive from looking at the cover and date of first printing. I was more than impressed, in fact; I was actually inspired to keep reading. I looked to see who the author was; as my friend entered, I said: "This is a load of Crock you're reading". He replied: "What are you talking about, that's great stuff." "I know", I said, "It's very inspiring; it's Father Clement Crock," pointing to the spine of the book. We then spent the evening talking about this exciting author, who was a simple parish priest from Ohio, ordained in 1917. He'd written a number of very basic books on the fundamentals of the Catholic faith. If the covers were new, no one would ever know they were written in the 30s and 40s. I was able to purchase a number of them, used, for less than $5 a book, each one of which smelled as if it had been on a shelf in a damp basement for the past 50 years.

I don't pretend to be able to equal or surpass someone like "the Crock", but I've been inspired to follow him, that is, to provide young people in particular with the basic teachings of the faith and the fundamental principles that underlie them.

There are so many such old and hidden treasures in used book stores all over the world collecting dust, enough to keep any Catholic busy for the rest of his or her life. These treasures are a small part of a vast and rich heritage, for anyone who has eyes to see past dates and dull covers.

I cannot add to this vast collection of treasures; all I can hope to do is open a few doors to this rich treasure house, a house much larger than the capacity of the imagination when we consider the entire history of the Church, but I am thinking only of the 20th century, and what is hidden in that period alone is significantly larger than what any one individual life span is capable to exploring adequately. For example, there is St. Edith Stein, Francois Xavier Durrwell, Caryll Houselander, Metropolitan Anthony, Father Romano Guardini, Father Ronald Knox, Blessed Columba Marmion, Dorothy Day, Father Louis Bouyer, Father G. Desbuquois, Father Reginald Garrigou-Lagrange, and more recently, Father Benedict Groeschel, Pope John Paul II, Pope Benedict XVI, etc. But one can look further to Jacques-Bénigne Bossuet, or St. Catherine of Siena, St. Theresa of Avila, St. John of the Cross, St. Thomas Aquinas, St. Anselm, St. Augustine, the Eastern spiritual writers in the volumes of *The Philokalia*, such as St. Maximos the Confessor, St. Mark the Ascetic, St. Diadochos of Photiki, etc.

Recently I read about a person who picked up a couple of Group of Seven paintings at a garage sale for $50 apiece. The paintings were worth hundreds of thousands of dollars. The seller obviously had no idea what he had in his garage. I would say most Catholics are like that seller; they have no idea what is theirs in the Church, and because of that, they often have no idea what is theirs outside the Church, because if all the treasures of wisdom and knowledge are hidden in the Person of Christ (Col 2, 3), then in him we are given the eyes to spot treasures of beauty, wisdom and knowledge outside the visible Church as well.

Those who have stopped searching have become bored, but a Catholic should never experience boredom; he shouldn't even know the meaning of the word. There is just too much that our older siblings have left us, and what they've left us is far more profound and insightful than much of what we're being left with today. The means by which we have access to these rich treasures is vastly superior, to be sure; but technology is only as valuable as the ends it serves, and technology does not provide the ends, it is only a means to an end. The ultimate end is eternal union with God, and the only ones who are going to help us to that end are the Lord's great servants who lived without these technological means, yet who were able to think and write without them at a level superior to what we are used to today. If I succeed in inspiring anyone to begin searching through this vast heritage that is ours in the Church, then I will have achieved what I set out to achieve.

Deacon Douglas McManaman studied Philosophy at St. Jerome's College in Waterloo, and Theology at the University of Montreal. He is a regular columnist for the *Canadian Messenger of the Sacred Heart* and writes regularly for *Catholic Insight Magazine*, *Lifeissues.net*, and the *Catholic Educator's Resource Center*. He has been interviewed twice on EWTN Radio, *The Good Fight* with Barbara McGuigan. He is a Permanent Deacon for the Archdiocese of Toronto and ministers to those who suffer from mental illness. He is the current chaplain for the Toronto Chapter of the Catholic Teachers Guild, and he has been teaching Religion and Philosophy to senior high school students for over 25 years. He is currently teaching at Father Michael McGivney Catholic Academy in Markham, Ontario, Canada. He is the past president of the Canadian Fellowship of Catholic Scholars.

Chapter 1: Theology and the Proclamation of the Kingdom of God

St. Anselm, a great theologian and philosopher of the 11th century, coined the phrase "fides quaerens intellectum" (faith seeking understanding). This is precisely what theology is: faith seeking understanding. As such, faith is the starting point of theology, in contrast to philosophy, which has as its starting point principles grasped by the natural light of reason. Thus, articles of faith—truths revealed by God in Sacred Scripture—are the first principles of the science of sacred theology. That is why in theology, the argument from authority is the strongest argument. In philosophy, however, the argument from authority is the weakest of all arguments. For example, to argue that "the soul is the substantial form of the body because Aristotle says so" is very weak. But the theological argument that "in baptism we enter into Christ's death, because St. Paul says so in the sixth chapter of his letter to the Romans," is the strongest argument one can make in theology. For the authority we are appealing to is God, who is Truth; and Scripture is inspired by God (1 Tim 3, 16). Theology thus works from the top down (from principles revealed by God and held by faith), while philosophy works from the bottom up (from first principles grasped by the natural light of reason).

But philosophy is a necessary tool and a useful "handmaiden" of theology. If we do not understand the basics of human reasoning, we are bound to make all sorts of mistakes when doing theology, and as St. Thomas, quoting Aristotle, points out: "a slight initial error eventually grows to vast proportions".[1] But the theological virtue of faith is the *sine qua non* of theology. If a person does not believe in the claims of Christ, if a person does not believe the essential message of Christ's proclamation of the kingdom, then it is not possible to do theology, understand it or appreciate it.

What is this message of Christ's proclamation of the kingdom of God? This is a good place to start. The first words out of Jesus' mouth at the start of his public ministry were "The time is fulfilled, and the kingdom of God is at hand; repent, and believe in the gospel" (Mk 1, 15). Very early on Jesus points out that the kingdom of heaven belongs to "the poor in spirit" (Mt, 5, 3), that is, to those who recognize their utter need for God. And the very notion of the "kingdom of God" is at the heart of all his parables. The meaning of "kingdom of God" is not easy to contain in a simple definition, but let's begin with an analogy from the political sphere.

A kingdom has nations under its dominion, and it is ruled ultimately by a king. Israel achieved the status of a kingdom, and it was the hope of the Jews that the Messiah would raise Israel to the status of a kingdom once again, with other nations subjugated and under its rule. And so a kingdom is established over and against an already existing kingdom, for example the Assyrians, Babylonians, Persians, or Romans. Historically, kingdoms have been established through war. The victors are thereby delivered from subjugation, that is, from slavery to the order of the fallen kingdom.

From a reading of the New Testament Scriptures, it is very clear that Jesus came to establish a kingdom. Hence, he was at war. But who was his enemy? Contrary to the expectations of his disciples, Jesus did not come to re-establish the kingdom of Israel as they understood it: "Lord, are you at this time going to restore the kingdom to Israel?" He answered them, "It is not for you to know the times or seasons that the Father has established by his own authority" (Acts 1, 6). The disciples had a difficult time understanding this: "From that time on, Jesus began to show his disciples that he must go to Jerusalem and suffer greatly from the elders, the chief priests, and the scribes, and be killed and on the third day be raised. Then Peter took him aside and began to rebuke him, "God forbid, Lord! No such thing shall ever happen to you." He turned and said to Peter, "Get behind me, Satan! You are an obstacle to me. You are thinking not as God does, but as human beings do" (Mt 16, 21-23).

In short, the Roman Empire was not Christ's enemy; it fell in the year 476 AD. Christ's enemy was far more ominous, and it was an enemy that man could not hope to defeat. Christ came to deliver man not from the slavery of a political regime, but from the slavery of sin and the dominion of death. Christ came to establish the kingdom of God over and against the kingdom of darkness. To understand this, we must return to one of the most important parts of Scripture, the allegorical account of the fall of man in the book of Genesis.

Angels and the Fall of Man

When reading the Scriptures, we must keep in mind that there is a distinction between an assertion and a proposition. What is asserted in Scripture is not always easy to discern, and neither is it something that can be fully explained from one angle alone. A Catholic relies on three sources in order to understand what is being asserted in Scripture, and these sources are **historical tradition**, the **teaching office of the Church**, and the entire context of **the Scriptures** themselves. Taking this allegory in Genesis literally inevitably misses the deeper theological meaning underlying it. From the point of view of historical tradition and the teaching office of the Church, the story of the fall of man was never proposed as a literal account, but an allegory that asserts a great deal about the fallen human condition.

We are all familiar with the story of the Fall, so there is no need to repeat it here. But the opening line speaks of "the serpent", which is "most cunning". One cannot enter into play with a serpent as one can play with a dog or cat. They are not capable of relating through play, and human beings seem to have a natural aversion to them. In this story, "the serpent" refers not to a literal animal, but to a personal being who is utterly devoid of play, one filled with a spirit of malice. For a person is an individual substance of a rational nature, but an animal, such as a lizard or snake, is not intelligent. The serpent in this story is intelligent and is a symbolic representation of a preternatural being. Let's focus for a moment on angels in order to more fully appreciate the very mission of Christ.

The word "preternatural" simply means "outside of nature". Man is the highest creature within the physical (natural) universe. He is the only creature in the universe who exists in the image and likeness of God (Gn 1, 26), that is, in the image of knowledge and love (mind and heart). Every other living creature is governed not by reason, but by a more or less sophisticated internal sense, the estimative sense, otherwise known as instinct. But even though man is the highest creature in the physical (natural) hierarchy of being, he is the lowest being on the hierarchy of intellectual creatures. Scripture speaks of this preternatural realm, the angelic realm: For example, in Daniel we read: "I was still occupied with this prayer, when Gabriel, the one whom I had seen before in vision, came to me in rapid flight at the time of the evening sacrifice. He instructed me in these words: "Daniel, I have now come to give you understanding..." (Dn 9, 21-22). In Isaiah we read: "Then I said, "Woe is me, I am doomed! For I am a man of unclean lips, living among a people of unclean lips; yet my eyes have seen the King, the Lord of Hosts!" Then one of the seraphim flew to me, holding an ember which he had taken with tongs from the altar. He touched my mouth with it. "See," he said, "now that this has touched your lips, your wickedness is removed, your sin purged" (Is 6, 5-7). In the New Testament we read: "...the harvest is the end of the age, and the harvesters are the angels" (Mt 13, 39); "The Son of Man will send his angels" (Mt 13, 40); "Thus it will be at the end of the age. The angels will go out and separate the wicked from the righteous..." (Mt 13, 49); "For the Son of Man will come with his angels in his Father's glory..." (Mt 16, 27); "See that you do not despise one of these little ones, for I say to you that their angels in heaven always look upon the face of my heavenly Father" (Mt 18, 10).

An angel is a pure spirit, an immaterial substance of a rational nature. A human person, on the other hand, is a material substance of a rational nature (a rational animal). French historian of philosophy Etienne Gilson calls man an "incarnated angel". As a pure intelligence, an angel is exceedingly more brilliant than the brightest human being. Human intelligence is historical and sluggish. As an example, consider that what students routinely do in math classes today took centuries for the most brilliant human intellects to discover, from Pythagoras to Descartes to Pascal to Russell. We look back and wonder why it took them so long. The reason is that the most brilliant among us are slow--what does that say for the rest of us?

But the mind of an angel is not historical and sluggish, for it is not subject to time; for time is the measure of movement, and as such is linked with the mutability of material substance. And so even the choices that are made by an angel do not take place in time, but rather within an indivisible aevum (eviternity).[2] An angel chooses at an instant whether it will position its entire existence towards God, or position itself in rebellion to the divine will. It must have this opportunity; for God, who is Love (1 Jn 4, 16), does not force anyone to love Him—to do so is contrary to the nature of love. As long as a human person exists in time, there is time for him to change his will, that is, to forfeit his friendship with God, or to finally choose friendship with God. The lives of some of the greatest saints tell of some of the most extraordinary conversions. But this is not so for an angel. The *aevum* is indivisible (unlike a minute, a second, or a split second), and the angel, whose choice is entirely free and enlightened, remains in his decision forever.

Now Scripture and tradition speak of an angel of the cherubim rank that fell through pride.[3] The word "cherubim" means "fullness of knowledge". According to Pseudo-Dionysius, the cherubim are the most intelligent of angels: "the serpent was the most cunning animal that the Lord God had made" (Gn 3, 1). Jesus speaks of the fall of Lucifer in a way that seems to call attention to the instantaneous character of his choice: "I have observed Satan fall like lightening from the sky" (Lk 10, 18). But we get a glimpse of the nature of his fall through the story of the fall. Here the "serpent" attempts to draw the proto-parents of the human race into the very current of his prideful and lying character: "You certainly will not die! No, God knows well that the moment you eat of it your eyes will be opened and you will be like God who knows what is good and what is bad" (3, 5).

The key to the meaning of this text lies in the symbolism of the "tree of knowledge of good and evil". Of course, Scripture is not referring to a literal tree, but rather to the possibility of a particular experience. Consider that childhood is characterized by dependency. A child depends upon adults, especially his parents, to teach him what is good from what is bad. Adulthood, on the contrary, is characterized by independence. The temptation to taste of the fruit from the tree of knowledge of good and evil is an ingenious and colorful way of representing the temptation to taste independence from God, that is, to be one's own god. In other words, as God is the measure of what is true and good, and as man is measured by the true and the good, this temptation seeks to reverse this order, by flipping it on its head, so to speak. This is precisely the sin of pride, the rejection of our status as children, dependent upon God and measured by something larger than ourselves. The proto-parents of the human race chose to succumb to this temptation, that is, they chose to be their own god.

What the circumstances surrounding this radical decision were, we can't even speculate. What is asserted through Scripture is that the first parents made a free and radical decision that would affect each of their offspring—since everything we do affects our offspring—,and the offspring of the first parents is the human race itself.

The three effects of this radical decision correspond to the loss of the three preternatural gifts that belonged to man in the state of Original Justice (bodily immortality, infused knowledge of God, and freedom from concupiscence). The human person was meant to live forever bodily, but death entered the world through sin (Rm 5, 12): "...he must not be allowed to put out his hand to take fruit from the tree of life also, and thus eat of it and live forever" (Gn 3, 22). And so, "from dust you came and to dust you shall return" (Gn 3, 19).

In the state of Original Justice, man had an infused knowledge of God, which was lost through sin. The account of the Fall reveals that as a result of sin, man is no longer at ease in God's presence, that is, in the presence of holiness: "When they heard the sound of the Lord God moving about in the garden at the breezy time of the day, the man and his wife hid themselves from the Lord God among the trees of the garden" (Gn 3, 8). In

7

other words, man can no longer correctly interpret God's advances. Thus, man lacks wisdom; for sin blinds the intellect. Hence, the second effect of original sin, the dulling of the mind.

Finally, original sin has brought it about that what is humanly good to do is now difficult: "…in pain shall you bring forth children…By the sweat of your face shall you get bread to eat" (Gn 3, 16-19). Thus, the third effect of original sin, traditionally referred to as concupiscence, is an inclination to sin, a tendency to selfishness. That is why virtue is difficult and vice is easy. It is easier to be unjust than it is to be just, and it is easier to be cowardly than it is to be brave; it is easier to be self-indulgent than it is to be temperate, and it is easier to be proud than it is to be humble. It is easier to be imprudent than it is to be prudent, and since prudence is the mother of the virtues, vice is easier than virtue.

Everybody is aware of the truth of this, for we readily see this disorder within ourselves. But God did not create man this way any more than Toyota designs cars to veer off the road with ease. This is a defect of human nature, a quasi-natural flaw that, according to divine revelation, has its roots in this historical act. It is difficult to appreciate the gravity of this first sin when we consider it merely from an intellectual point of view. Perhaps we get a deeper sense of its seriousness when we consider how twisted this world really is. But even here, at this point, not everyone can see the twisted nature of the world in which we live. Vice blinds the mind. But this moral woundedness and emotional disorder has led to terrible injustice and suffering. Consider the amount of suffering with which history is filled. One day's newspaper is almost too much for most of us to handle in one sitting. It shouldn't take a great deal of research to recognize that there is something terribly wrong with the human situation, that is, that there is something terribly wrong with human beings.

But the most important text in chapter three of Genesis begins at verse 15:

> Because you have done this, you shall be banned from all the animals and from all the wild creatures; on your belly shall you crawl, and dust shall you eat all the days of your life. I will put enmity between you and the woman, and between your offspring and hers; He will strike at your head, while you strike at his heel.

Here we are given a sense of the fall of Satan (on your belly shall you crawl) and the alienation which he suffers (you shall be banned from...). The Evil One feeds on death (dust), that is, he has lost the life of divine grace. But most importantly, this text reveals a conflict, a tension that will exist between "the woman" and "the serpent". The woman in this text cannot be the first woman, for her heart is in line with that of the serpent; for she listened to him. There will come a woman whose heart will not belong to darkness, a woman whose offspring will strike at the head of the serpent; the image of a foot crushing the head while the serpent "strikes at his heel" suggests a victory. But where there is victory, there was war, and where there is war, there is an aggressor and a defender. Typically the aggressor is unjust, but in this case the aggressor attempts to reclaim what was rightfully his in the first place. This war is between the serpent and its offspring (all those who choose to belong to darkness) and the offspring of "the woman". And so there is a sense in which, according to biblical thinking, the world—prescinding from the redemption of Christ—belongs to the Evil One, who is referred to by John as "the ruler of this world" (Jn 12, 31; 16, 11; Rev 12, 9-13; Lk 4, 6).

Christians believe that Jesus is the offspring of "the woman"; for on two occasions he refers to his own mother as "woman". First, at the wedding in Cana: "When the wine ran short, the mother of Jesus said to him, "They have no wine." And Jesus said to her, "Woman, how does your concern affect me? My hour has not yet come" (Jn 2, 3-4). Secondly, on Calvary: "When Jesus saw his mother and the disciple there whom he loved, he said to his mother, "Woman, behold, your son." Then he said to the disciple, "Behold, your mother" (Jn 19, 26-27). It is the fruit of her womb that is being grafted back onto the tree, the wood of the cross, the new tree of life, and this is his victory over the one who has the power of death; for he has come to "destroy the one who has the power of death, that is, the devil, and free those who through fear of death had been subject to slavery all their life" (Heb 2, 14; 1 Jn 3, 8). He came to substitute the kingdom of his Father for that of darkness (See 1 Co 15, 24-28): "He delivered us from the power of darkness and transferred us to the kingdom of his beloved Son, in whom we have redemption, the forgiveness of sins" (Col 1, 13).

And the gospels present Jesus' public life as a battle against "the ruler of this world of darkness". The battle begins in the desert where for the first time since Paradise, "the Son of Adam, the Son of God" (Lk 3, 38) finds himself face to face with the devil. And the miracles of Christ are precisely signs that the kingdom of darkness has come to an end (Lk 10, 13-20). For sin brought death, but Jesus raises both Lazarus and Jairus's daughter (Mk 5, 21; Jn 11, 1-44) from the dead, and he himself conquers death in his resurrection on Easter Sunday. From henceforth he holds the keys to death and the netherworld (Rev 1, 18). As biblical scholar Xavier Leon Dufour writes, the struggle "reaches its paroxysm at the hour of the passion. Luke consciously links the passion to the temptation (Lk 4, 13; 22, 53), and John underlines the role of Satan in it (Jn 13, 2. 27; 14, 30; cf Lk 22, 3. 31) only to proclaim his final defeat".4

This is precisely the good news of the kingdom of God: deliverance from the slavery of sin and from the power of death is ours in the Person of Christ. *The message of the gospel is thus a message of hope; for it is a message of salvation.* The proclamation of the kingdom of God is not the proclamation of a moral doctrine, but the proclamation of **a victory**, a victory over the kingdom of despair and its ruler, and the establishment of the reign of hope and the throne of a new king.

Chapter 2: Redemption and the Virtue of Religion

Original sin is a state in which each human person is born, a state that was created by an original and free decision. Each member of the human community is born without the supernatural life of divine grace. Man (Adam) is no longer in "God's favor" (grace), for he has separated himself from God. Thus he no longer shares in the life of God, and grace is precisely a sharing in the divine life. Man has a share in his own life naturally, but the life of God is supra-natural, and there is nothing that man can do to achieve the life of grace; for it would require that he exceed the capacity of his nature. To do that by virtue of the principles of his nature is contradictory. Furthermore, there is nothing he can do to merit grace, for it is not even possible for him to merit existence in the natural order; and, it is only through grace that man can rise above his inclination to sin and selfishness. So how is man to acquire a sharing in the divine life, which he lost through sin? How is man to repair or make reparation for what he has done? In short, how can he do justice for his own sin?

It has always been the faith of the Church that man simply cannot restore what he has lost. In other words, man cannot save himself.

It is easier for a camel to pass through the eye of a needle than for someone rich to enter the kingdom of God." They were more astonished than ever, saying to one another, "in that case, who can be saved?" Jesus gazed at them and said, "By human resources it is impossible, but not for God: because for God everything is possible (Mk 10, 25-27)

It is this impossibility that I would like to focus on for a while, in order to more fully appreciate the fittingness of the Incarnation, and I will do so by

12

Basic Catholicism

considering this from an angle that was made popular by
St. Anselm in the eleventh century, but which has been
and continues to be widely misunderstood.

Justice is the virtue by which we perpetually will to
render to another his due. But there are situations in
which we cannot fully satisfy the debt that is owed.
Such situations call for special virtues allied with justice.
For example, we cannot fully satisfy the debt we owe
our parents. To keep this as simple as possible, consider
the parents who bring up their children well. How can
such parents be repaid for the good that they do for
their children and for civilization? The virtue that
responds to this situation is piety, the virtue by which we
render due honor to our parents. Consider also the debt
we owe to the civil community as a whole; for we are the
beneficiaries of the labor of hundreds of thousands of
people; we couldn't begin to satisfy the debt we owe to
these unknown benefactors. But patriotism is the virtue
that responds to this particular situation, the virtue by
which we render due honor and worship to country.

Now, everything we have and are is nothing less
than sheer gift; for God is the First Cause of all that is.
Whatever is, whether a thought, an act of the will, or a
carbon atom, is caused ultimately by God (He Who Is).
We cannot fully render to God our debt to Him for the
purely gratuitous gift of human existence, which is a
communication of His goodness in which we were made
to share. The virtue of religion is that part of justice that
responds to this situation in which every person finds
himself. In other words, there is a natural duty to be
religious (not only a supernatural duty rooted in
baptism). Being religious is not an option alongside
others, to be chosen according to one's personal
inclination or preference. It is a duty, the most serious
demand of justice, to attempt as far as one is able to
render to God what is His due.

13

The most basic response to gift is to receive it with
thanks. But a truly thankful person will choose to repay
the gift as much as it is in his power to do so. The
natural virtue of religion (the most perfect part of
justice) disposes us to make God the very center of our
lives. There is nothing we do not owe God, for we owe
Him everything, and every attempt at repayment
presupposes the gift that we are attempting to repay. In
other words, if I am to attempt to render God thanks by
acts of worship, prayer, and almsgiving, etc., I must
"exist" and be preserved in existence in order to do so.
That preservation is itself sheer gift. Hence, gift is
always prior to every one of our attempts at a thankful
response to it.

But when we commit an offense against someone,
we create a debt towards the offended party. Justice is
the full rendering of that debt. Now sin creates a debt in
regards to God that is over and above the natural debt
already owing Him. If we cannot fully render the latter,
how can we hope to satisfy the former? Sin creates a
debt, in other words, that infinitely exceeds our power to
satisfy. Hence, man cannot make up for sin. Man
cannot save himself. Or, what amounts to the same
thing, man cannot justify himself.

Only God can satisfy this debt that infinitely
exceeds our capacity to satisfy it because God is
omnipotent, that is, God is not limited by potentiality.
He is existentially infinite. But God is the offended
party, and so it is not incumbent upon Him to make
satisfaction for sin any more than a victim of fraud
ought to make up for the fraud committed against him.

The Trinity and the Incarnation of the Son

The New Testament reveals that Christ is precisely
God's solution to this impossible situation: "...for all
things are possible for God" (Mk 10, 27). Jesus reveals

God as Trinity. Prior to the coming of Christ, God was not understood to be triune. But the New Testament speaks of this Trinity of Persons, the Father, the Son, and the Holy Spirit. God is three Persons, but one Nature. Now, we know that God's nature is "to be" (God is Subsistent Existence Itself), and so there is one God, not three Gods. But mysteriously, this one divine being is a Trinity of Persons. The first Person of the Trinity is the Father, the Second Person of the Trinity is the Son, and the third Person of the Trinity is the Holy Spirit.

Let us focus on the Second Person of the Trinity for a moment. Consider the first creation story. God said: "Let there be light, and there was light...God said, "Let there be a dome in the middle...so it happened...God said, "Let the water under the sky be gathered into...so it happened...God said: "Let us make man in our image, after our likeness..." In other words, all things came to be through God's spoken word. Everything has being simply by virtue of the fact that God knows it and wills it into existence. God is not measured by the real, but is the measure of "what is".

The gospel of John focuses on this point of creation. He writes: "In the beginning was the Word. The Word was with God, and the Word was God" (Jn 1, 1). In other words, this Word (Logos) who is God is also distinct from God (with God). And "through him all things came to be. Not one thing came to be without him" (Jn 1, 3). This parallels the first chapter of Genesis in which God says "Let there be..." The Word, who was "in the beginning", is the Son, the only Son of the Father, and the Word entered, unrecognized, into the darkness of this world:

> The light shines in the darkness, and the darkness has not overcome it...He came to what was his own, but his own did not accept him...And the Word became

flesh and made his dwelling among us, and we saw his glory, the glory as of the Father's only Son, full of grace and truth" (Jn 1, 5; 11-14).

Hence, Jesus is the Person of the Son. He is not two Persons, but one Person; but this one Person has two natures: one divine (the Word was with God and the Word was God), and one human (and the Word became flesh). In other words, Jesus is God-man. He is the Father's spoken Word uttered in history. And so everything that the Father can say about Himself is spoken in the Person of Jesus (Logos).5

It is this "becoming flesh" that is God's solution to the impossibility of man's self-justification. As man, Jesus can step forward on behalf of the entire human community (on behalf of Adam) and offer a sacrifice of reparation for the sin which infinitely exceeds man's ability to satisfy, but which is incumbent upon man to do so. As God the Son, his sacrifice has an infinite value. For he chose to offer his blood, and for the Jews the life was in the blood: "Since the life of the living body is in its blood, I have made you put it on the altar, so that atonement may thereby be made for your own lives, because it is the blood, as the seat of life, that makes atonement" (Lv 17, 11-12). Jesus came to offer his life, to make atonement, that is, to reconcile the world to Himself: "There is a baptism with which I must be baptized, and how great is my anguish until it is accomplished!" (Lk 12, 50). His life (blood) is the life of the Person of the Son. Because the Son is divine, his offering alone can cancel the debt of sin; for it is a sacrifice whose value is limitless. His offering is an act of atonement, an act of justification, in short, an act of re-creation.

The sacrifice of the cross is the perfect fulfillment of the requirement of justice; it is the perfect act of religion offered to the Father on our behalf. The cross is our justification, because it is the perfect act of justice:

> But God proves his love for us in that while we were still sinners Christ died for us. How much more then, since we are now justified by his blood, will we be saved through him from the wrath. Indeed, if, while we were enemies, we were reconciled to God through the death of his Son, how much more, once reconciled, will we be saved by his life (Rm 5, 8-10).

It is **not** that the Father had to punish mankind for sin, and so He punished Christ who substitutes himself for us. Such a misunderstanding, which was and is very prevalent, is rooted in a narrowing of the idea of justice to that kind which is restitution. Christ came not to receive a just punishment from God, but to be the fullness of justice for our sake. He is the perfection of that part of justice that is the virtue of religion, and so in Him we have the forgiveness of sins. His act is a sacrifice whose effect embraces the entire span of human history, because it is the sacrifice of the eternal Person of the Son. And so it is in Him that all human persons find the life of grace. And so it is true to say that there is only one place and one moment in history where the debt man owes to God is fully paid, and that was on Calvary in the early first century; and because it is the sacrifice of the Son who is eternal, it is an act that endures throughout history.₆

The resurrection is the Father's acceptance of Christ's offering of Himself on our behalf; for his was an acceptable sacrifice. And the resurrection is precisely the good news of the gospel. The Greek word "evangelion" is a term that was used exclusively in connection with extraordinarily good news, in particular the good news of a military victory, or the birth of a king. In Christ we have both. His death is his victory over sin, and his resurrection is his victory over death: "the life who was the light of the world" entered into death, transforming it into life. Death no longer has the final word over our lives. The Word has the final word over our lives, and how happy are those who will hear in the end: "Come, you that are blessed by my Father, inherit the kingdom prepared for you from the foundation of the world" (Mt 25, 34).

The Gratuitous Nature of the Redemption

One student of mine recently asked me: "If God the Son joined Himself to a human nature and offered the sacrifice of reparation on our behalf, why is it that it goes unacknowledged by most people? She could not understand how it could possibly be true that so important a Person as the Person of the Son could enter into the darkness of this world, suffer and die for us without an acknowledgment equal to the weight of the deed. Most people go on their merry way as beneficiaries of a redemption that they are probably not even aware of. And how many of us who are so aware acknowledge it or appreciate it enough?

Her insight underscores the utter generosity of the deed. Our redemption is sheer gift, and it does not depend upon our acknowledgment of it. We have been reconciled to God whether we are aware of it or not, and so many graces proceed from that redemption that make our lives so much richer in meaning, and these graces are communicated to us without our having earned them and often without our being explicitly aware of them: "From his fullness we have all received grace upon grace" (Jn 1, 16).

But Christian conversion is precisely the recognition of that redemption and an opening of the heart to a new birth. One is no longer divided, but given over to the kingdom, despite the fact that one's love is still relatively impure. The difference is that he does not settle for such imperfection and division, but spends the rest of his life trying to achieve a completely undivided love: "Blessed are the pure in heart, they shall see God" (Mt 5, 8). It is possible to speak of a relatively unconverted Catholic, one whose heart is divided, who has not turned his eye to the heavenly city, but who has not entirely rejected it either. Such a precarious situation will not last too long, though, because man is a creature of habit. But such lives can be compared to the child who takes his parents for granted and is focused almost exclusively on the gifts he receives from them. Hopefully he will come to realize that his parents are themselves the gift. And if, after they have died, he keeps anything that they at one time had given him, he does so not for the sake of the thing itself, but rather because it came from them. He has learned to love the person behind the gift. But it is not inevitable that he will do so. Some people never learn to love God over his gifts, and such people will never be as happy as they can be. And some, like the child spoiled rotten with avarice, will choose never to acknowledge the giver of all that they've been given. And God loves these latter so much that He will indeed allow them to reject Him for all eternity.

But the more we turn our gaze upon the Word made flesh, the more we succeed in becoming the persons we are intended to be. This is because all things came to be through the Word, including ourselves. The Word is our origin and end. We discover who we are in our origin and in our end, that is, in the Word who spoke us into existence.

A Partial Reply to Christopher Hitchens

Recently I heard only a portion of a debate in which atheist Christopher Hitchens argues that the doctrine of "vicarious atonement" is an immoral and highly dangerous one (the teaching that God the Son joins a human nature in order to offer himself to the Father on our behalf, that we may attain the forgiveness of our sins). He argues that to take a guilty man's place of punishment, for example, to go to prison in his stead or to submit to execution on his behalf, is repugnant to the very idea of justice; for the criminal alone can pay his debt, not the innocent man. If I who am innocent decide to go to prison or the scaffold instead of the killer, then I cooperate with evil and perpetuate an unjust state of affairs—the killer remains at large, while an innocent man is in prison or worse, put to death.

But that is not an analogous case that accurately illustrates the doctrine of Christ's redemption.

First, if someone is indebted to me, it is not repugnant to the very idea of justice for me to forgive that debt. That is, rather, an act of mercy; and mercy transcends justice. So, if someone owes me a debt so great that he cannot repay it fully, I can remit the debt, cancel it, and bear the loss, if I so choose, especially if my purpose in forgiving that debt is to communicate the love I have for my debtor.

God can cancel our debt if He so chooses. And we, the human race as a whole, have a debt to Him that we cannot fully repay. He has chosen to remit that debt. But He also chose to remit it in a way that visibly manifests His love for us who are, out of His ninety-nine sheep, the single sheep that has gone astray (Lk 15, 4-7). But He remits this debt in a way that fulfils both the requirements of justice and at the same time reveals His infinite mercy.

Secondly, it is not unjust for the human race as a whole to seek out God's forgiveness for its own sin. The problem is that the human race as a whole can do nothing about this debt. It cannot pay the debt and make satisfaction for sin, because sin against God is of infinite gravity. But it would be fitting for one member of the human race to come forward on behalf of all of humanity and offer something in reparation, as a lawyer steps forward to represent a corporation, or an ambassador represents a country.

So God provides the solution. He joins a human nature to Himself: Jesus is two natures (human and divine), but one Person (the Person of the Son), and he (Jesus) acts on our behalf, as an ambassador acts on behalf of a nation. He is our voice. Now that is fitting; for he is truly man, a member of the human race.

But he is also fully God, and so what he offers, namely his own life, has a value that is not limited. Unlike anything we can offer, the value of Christ's offering is commensurate to the debt of sin, which is of infinite gravity. There is nothing repugnant to justice here. It is an act of mercy, a gift; his sacrificial act manifests the divine love for man, and it cancels the debt of sin so that the life of God (divine grace) can once again flow through the veins of humanity, justifying each person who freely chooses to cooperate with that grace.

Hitchens' argument does not stand because his analogy is a false one. For me to take the place of a killer and go to prison in his stead is indeed repugnant to justice because the criminal has committed an injustice against the civil community as a whole (as well as a sin against God), not against me personally. His sin is not for me to forgive, for it is not against me personally. My going to prison does not balance the scales of justice, because it leaves intact an unjust state of affairs—the killer is still on the loose. A more accurate analogy is the cancellation of a debt owed to me personally by one individual person, or an individual family, a debt that cannot be fully remitted. To continue the analogy, a member of that family steps forward to offer a sacrifice of reparation, on behalf of that family, in order to remit the debt. Doing so, of course, is impossible, and so we are in an impossible situation—unless I, who have an unlimited source of funds, can somehow become a member of that family and make that offering myself, so that my mercy would be visible to each member of that family.

Chapter 3: Matter and the Sacraments

Divine grace, as we said earlier, is a participation in the divine life. The human person is not born in a state of grace. In other words, grace is not natural to human beings, but is rather a supernatural quality (habit or disposition) infused by God. God is present to everything naturally as first existential cause of a thing's act of being, but he is not present to everything supernaturally, that is, through the habit of grace. Grace is God's self-communication, a self-communication that is over and above His natural presence. If this was not the case, it would be impossible to speak of the sacred. For the word "sacred" means "set apart". As an example, consider that if God is no more present in the tabernacle than He is in a garbage can, then a chapel is not a sacred place.

We are made holy through this supra-natural presence, and it is this divine favor that Christ came to restore. This favor is ours in Him, to the degree that we share in his perfect act of religion (the sacrifice of the cross): "Whoever wishes to come after me must deny himself, take up his cross, and follow me" (Mk 8, 34). In a sense, this is what is meant by the kingdom of God: the redemptive presence of God, through the power of his Holy Spirit. The world now belongs to Christ, eternal life is ours for the asking, and it is in Him that we have the forgiveness of sins. We will taste death, but if we die in Him, we will also live with Him: "If, then, we have died with Christ, we believe that we shall also live with him" (Rm 6, 8). We still suffer from a dulling of the intellect, but the more we grow in grace, the more we share in the personal gifts of the Holy Spirit, especially wisdom, knowledge and understanding. And we still suffer from an inclination to sin, but we have all that we need to rise above this tendency, namely divine grace: "God is faithful and will not let you be tempted

beyond your strength; but with the temptation he will
also provide a way out, so that you may be able to bear
it" (1 Cor 10, 13).

But man is a unity of spirit and matter. In other
words, he is a psychosomatic unity. Matter plays a very
important role in every aspect of our lives, and this
includes the spiritual life. Material substances are
existing natures which we come to understand not
directly, but through sense perception. More
specifically, we understand the nature of things gradually
as we observe their activity. This is in accordance with
the psychosomatic nature of the human person. That is
why the spiritual life, if it is to accord with the nature of
the human person, must also be intimately bound up
with matter. This is another way of implying that the
spiritual life is sacramental. For the Catholic, grace is
normally communicated sacramentally, **through the
instrumentality of matter**, that is, through matter that
is both visible and tangible, such as water, oil, or bread
and wine.

Baptism and the Gifts of the Holy Spirit

The sacraments are the activity of Christ's Mystical
Body, the Church. More specifically, sacraments are
channels of grace. Each sacrament is a unity of sign
(matter) and word (form). For example, the matter of
the sacrament of baptism is water; for water is a natural
sign of purity, cleansing, and new life. What makes
baptism to be "what it is" is the form or words: "I
baptize you in the name of the Father, and of the Son,
and of the Holy Spirit." Water is the most fitting sign
for baptism because water is a natural sign of life; for life
depends upon water. It is also an apt sign of death in
that water is the most powerful force in nature—too
much water drowns. Baptism is both a death and a
resurrection to new life. Through the waters of baptism,

a person dies to the old Adam and becomes a new creation: "Or are you unaware that we who were baptized into Christ Jesus were baptized into his death? We were indeed buried with Him through baptism into death, so that, just as Christ was raised from the dead by the glory of the Father, we too might live in newness of life" (Rm 6, 3-4).

This does not mean that grace cannot be communicated outside of baptism; but the graces of baptism effect a radical conversion or regeneration in the human person. One receives a spirit of adoption, and one thereby becomes a new creation: "So whoever is in Christ is a new creation: the old thing have passed away; behold, new things have come" (2 Cor 5, 17). The baptized is cleansed from Original Sin.

Baptism also infuses the theological virtues of faith, hope, and charity. These are not natural virtues that one can cultivate on one's own efforts. Faith is pure gift, and there is nothing we can do to earn or acquire it; and it is the greatest gift that a human person can receive; for there is nothing else by which a person may enter the fullness of heaven. And although a person cannot not give to himself faith, he alone is the cause of his own loss of faith. There is no tragedy greater than that of a person who was given the gift of faith as sheer gift, but who lost it through his own indifference. That is why faith must be nourished through prayer, the sacramental life, and study.

Faith is a gift that gives us the power to believe what God has revealed about Himself and which exceeds the grasp of human reason. But if a person is given that grace, he or she has to choose to cooperate with it. But some people find that very difficult and even refuse. The irony is that they have no problem trusting the media, their colleagues, their bosses, their friends, etc.

The theological virtue of faith is a decision to believe Christ and his unique claims—and he made some very unique claims. For example: "I am the Way, the Truth, and the Life. No one can come to the Father except through me"; "Anyone who has seen me has seen the Father"; "I am the resurrection. Anyone who believes in me, even though he dies, will live, will never die." "Sky and earth will pass away, but my words will never pass away"; "Before Abraham was, I AM"; "I and the Father are one"; "I am the bread of life"; "It is my Father's will that whoever sees the Son and believes in him should have eternal life, and that I should raise that person up on the last day"; "Anyone who eats my flesh and drinks my blood has eternal life, and I shall raise that person up on the last day". These are astounding claims.

If Jesus is no more than a man, a mere human being, these claims are simply outrageous. It was C.S. Lewis who made the point that if Jesus is not who he claimed to be, then he is insane, or he is a liar. Our sanity is measured by the distance that exists between who we claim to be and who we really are, so if I say I'm the reincarnation of Napoleon, you can be assured that I'm insane. If Jesus is not the Son of God, one in being with the Father, and he did not know that, but claimed to be, then he's more insane. If he knows he's not God the Son but claimed to be, he's the biggest liar in human history.

If you read a gospel and find that Jesus does not have the persona of an insane man or a liar, then the only other option is that he is who he says he is, namely, the Way, the Truth, and the Life, the eternal Son of God in the flesh, the Resurrection and the Life, and that he who believes in him will live forever. That is how far human reason can go in showing that it is reasonable to put your faith in the Person of Christ. That doesn't prove he is God the Son, but it takes us pretty close and makes the leap of faith that much easier.

Thomas the Apostle knew Jesus, he witnessed his miracles, he heard Jesus foretell his death and resurrection on the third day, but he refused to believe the testimony of the disciples that they'd seen the risen Lord. He had to see for himself. We can detect a slight rebuke in Jesus' words to him for his stubbornness: "Do not doubt but believe". Thomas then declares his faith, but Jesus says: "You believe because you have seen; Blessed are those who believe without having seen." That must have been somewhat of a humiliating experience for Thomas; although Thomas is an Apostle, Christ is saying that there are others who will have greater merit, because they will choose to believe without evidence.

St. Catherine of Siena speaks so often about the "light of faith". There is an interior light, a knowledge that is generated by the act of faith. It comes after the decision to take that risk and believe Christ. St. Augustine said "believe in order to understand", not the other way around. If you wait to make an act of faith until you have enough intellectual understanding and assurance, you will never make the act of faith. God eventually rewards the decision to believe with an interior understanding, which is a gift of the Holy Spirit, but not before that decision.

Jesus said it himself: "Father, I praise you for having kept these truths from the learned and the sophisticated and have revealed them to mere children". It takes the heart of a child to believe, and the Lord said: "Unless you change and become as little children, you will never enter the kingdom of heaven". People have a hard time with childhood; they don't want to be children again. They want to appear and feel sophisticated, and so faith is difficult. The result is they just plod through life, on the ground, like a turtle, weighed down by its shell, and they never experience the exhilaration of flying. With faith we are given wings, and we fly, which can be scary at first, but it is a marvelous thing to be carried along by the Lord, and to come to know through experience the flame of the divine love, enkindled as it is by the wood of the cross. It's a marvelous thing to eventually experience the flame of that love, that divine presence in the deepest center of the soul. When you've experienced that living flame of the divine love, nothing matters anymore except communicating that flame to others. But there's no experiencing that without actually getting on that road to the center of that interior castle of the soul where God dwells and is waiting for us. It is supernatural faith, that childlike trusting in Christ, that allows us to begin making our way there. It's a long road inward, but without allowing ourselves to be led by the hand in a spirit of faith and trust, we'll never get there. But if we make it to the center, we will know a joy and a peace that this world simply cannot give to us, and there's nothing in this world that we'll take in exchange for it.

Baptism also confers the seven personal gifts of the Holy Spirit: wisdom, knowledge, understanding, counsel, piety, fortitude and fear of God. These too are not natural gifts—although they do have their natural counterparts. For example, Aristotle was profoundly wise, but he did not have the **wisdom** that is the gift of the Holy Spirit, which is profound insight into the things of God. One need not have a university education to receive a sharing in this gift. In fact, this gift is an effect of the theological virtue of charity (loving God under the aspect of personal friendship). Love begets knowledge, for the more we love a person, the more we desire to know them, and friends have a more intimate knowledge of one another than do others who do not enjoy such friendship. St. Therese of Lisieux, who entered the convent of Lisieux at 15 and died when she was only 24 years of age, had a very profound sharing in the gift of wisdom. To read her letters that she wrote in her early 20s, one gets the impression that the author had spent a good sixty years on the road of the spiritual life.

The gift of **knowledge** enables a person to see the hand of divine providence in every day occurrences. Where before a person would regard an occurrence as a mere coincidence, faith opens up a whole new perspective on life; one readily sees that God is intimately involved in our everyday lives, providentially ordering things for the best: "We know that all things work for good for those who love God, who are called according to his purpose" (Rm 8, 28). Mother Teresa of Calcutta had a rather profound sharing in this gift, for in her writings she very often calls attention to the hand of providence in her day to day life and the lives of her sisters.

Understanding is the gift by which we are given understanding of the mysteries of our faith. This does not necessarily imply that the person will be able to explain the mysteries, but there exists a certain grasp and recognition of the truth of these mysteries, such as the Trinity, the Incarnation, the Eucharist, etc. For example, sometimes a person who has never taken a theology course in his/her life will sense that there is something wrong with the homily that is being delivered. They may not know what exactly, but they know that something is amiss. This is the gift of understanding at work.

Counsel is that gift whereby a person is given the ability to discern that course of action most in accordance with God's will. Of course, no one has a perfect sharing in this gift, but as one grows spiritually, as one grows in the virtues of faith, hope, and charity, one grows in the gifts, especially counsel. St. Catherine of Siena was said to have had a strong gift of counsel and was often consulted by Popes in the fourteenth century. She too had an astounding gift of wisdom, for she only lived for thirty three years, but to read *The Dialogue*, which she wrote when she was 31, one inevitably has the impression that the author is well advanced in years.

Piety in the natural order is that virtue whereby we render due honor to our parents and country. In the order of grace, the gift of piety is that by which we render due honor to the Church, Christ's Mystical Body, and to Mary, the Blessed Mother who is, by virtue of our incorporation into Christ's Mystical Body, our mother; for Jesus received his body from his mother. If we are one body in Him, she too becomes our mother. And the fourth commandment is to honor one's father and mother. In imitation of Christ, we have a duty to honor Mary. Piety also includes devotion to the communion of saints, who are our older siblings that have gone before us, but who are still in communion with us. They can intercede for us and will do so if we ask them. We can come to know these saints while we are here, through devotion to them, and by studying their lives.

Fortitude also has its natural counterpart. It is the virtue that moderates the emotions of fear and daring so that we may achieve the ends required by justice, ends that are often difficult to achieve and give rise to fear. But supernatural ends proposed by faith are even more difficult to achieve. In fact, they are simply impossible to achieve without the theological virtues. The martyrs of the Church all had the gift of fortitude. Consider St. Thomas More, who had a wife and four children, an estate in Chelsea, and a solid political career. He refused to take the oath of succession that declared King Henry VIII the head of the Church of England, because as a Catholic he believed that the head of the visible Church was the successor of Peter (Pope), and not a king. He was committed to the tower of London for two years for not taking the oath of succession, with the annotation that he acted ungratefully and unkindly to the King, his benefactor. It was More's understanding that if he was to be found guilty of treason, he would be hanged drawn and quartered. This means he would be hanged in the normal way, but cut down while still conscious. The genitals would then be cut off and the stomach slit open. The intestines would then be removed and burned before him. The other organs would then be torn out and finally the head would be cut off, and the body divided into four quarters. The King had mercy at the last minute and commuted the sentence to beheading. But in the 16th century, 105 Catholic martyrs were hanged drawn and quartered at Tyburn in London for refusing to recognize the official religion of the day. If More had chosen, for the sake of his family, to take the oath of succession and declare Henry the head of the Church of England, he would have been immediately restored to his former status. But integrity of conscience was of greater value than any temporal advantage. More could not have remained faithful to his conscience without the supernatural gift of fortitude.

In the 17th century, in Canada, St. Jean de Brebeuf knew that he would likely die a horrible death at the hands of the Iroquois, but he committed his life to proclaiming the good news of the resurrection nonetheless. When captured, his eyes were gouged out and red hot coals were put in their place, his lips and nose were cut off, chunks of his thigh were cut off, fried and eaten, he was scalped and then "baptized" with boiling water in mockery of the sacrament, he was forced to wear a necklace of red hot hatchets, and finally his feet were cut off. The Indians were so impressed with his fortitude (for he suffered "like a rock") that they cut out his heart, drank the blood while it was still warm, and ate his heart, believing that by doing so they would receive his spirit of courage.

What was it that enabled the martyrs to willingly give their lives and endure the most horrible torments? They knew something that most of us do not; they had a faith so real, a hope so alive and a love so strong that they would willingly endure unspeakable suffering for the honor and glory of God. These are just two illustrations of the gift of fortitude.

Finally, the **fear of God**, which Scripture says is the beginning of wisdom. The gift of fear is, at least initially, a reverent fear of the divine justice. Traditionally, it has been divided into servile fear and filial fear. Servile fear inclines a person to reject sin out of a fear of punishment, whether temporal or eternal. Filial fear, on the other hand, inclines a person to reject sin more out of a fear of offending the beloved, namely God. Indeed, the latter is higher and nobler, but the latter does not displace the former. Filial fear does not supplant servile fear. Rather, the more a person grows in the love of God—and thus filial fear—, the more refined does servile fear become.

The reason is that as we grow in the knowledge of God's mercy, we grow, simultaneously in the knowledge of our own frailty and proclivity to sin, for His mercy bears upon our sins. And as we grow in an understanding of God's pure generosity, we begin to appreciate more the seriousness of sin. Joined to an awareness of our own frailty and dependency upon divine grace, we are led to pray for the gift of perseverance within a spirit of hope, which includes a spirit of fear that recognizes what we truly deserve. Indeed, the saint really fears the damage that his sins will do to himself as well as to others.

But it has become rather fashionable to redefine the "fear of God" as an experience of "awe". The Hebrew word for "fear", however, is *yare*, which does not mean awe or wonder, but fear or dread. Awe describes a very different experience than that of fear. This past month I stood before a number of 17th century paintings at the National Gallery of Art in Washington, D.C. The experience was one of awe and intense wonder, not fear. Fear is an entirely different emotion, one that bears upon an impending evil that is judged to be insurmountable.

Moreover, awe is not a starting point or a beginning, but a conclusion, an end, a quality that is acquired after a long period of labor. A person does not begin a course in Art or Music Appreciation with a fully developed sense of awe and wonder, but acquires an appreciation of a particular style of music or period of art after spending much time studying it and its place within history. How much more is awe at the divine majesty a conclusion, an end, a perfection acquired after many years of reflecting on the mystery of God's perfections, such as His omniscience, omnipotence, and His universal providence?

Fear, on the other hand, is a beginning: "The fear (*yare*) of the Lord is the beginning of wisdom" (Ps. 111, 10; Prv. 1, 7). The object of this fear is precisely the divine anger: "Who knows the fury of your anger or your indignation toward those who should fear (*yare*) you" (Ps 90, 11). Indeed, the fear of the Lord is a kind of reverence, but such reverence cannot be understood except in light of fear. The more we reverence something, the more we fear losing it. The more a person reverences his salvation, the more he will fear losing it (servile fear), and the more a person reverences God, the more he will fear offending Him (filial fear).

Awe towards God is not the beginning of wisdom, but a sign of wisdom acquired. But fear is the beginning of decisions that are wise and life giving. I have taught some young people in the past who have had absolutely no fear of God, servile or otherwise. Despite its imperfection, servile fear would have done these kids a great deal of good. Those pastors who refuse to preach on the real possibility of hell do the Church a great disservice. It is a mistake to assume that most people are beyond the level of servile fear. Very few ever grow beyond this level, and refusing to call attention to the existence of hell does not and will not take anyone beyond servile fear to a higher fear, rooted in genuine love. Ironically, this neglect does the reverse. Perhaps that is why Christ so often spoke of hell (Cf. Mt 5, 22; Mt 5, 30; Mt 7, 13; Mt 7, 19; Mt 7, 21-23; Mt 10, 39; Mt 11, 23-24; Mt 12, 37; Mt 13, 30; Mt 13, 40-43; Mt 13, 49-50; Mt 21, 40-41; Mt 22, 13-14; Mt 23, 15; Mt 23, 33; Mt 24, 50-51; Mt 25, 11-12; Mt 25, 30; Mt 25, 31-46).

Sweetening the harder points of the Gospel might appear more positive and inviting, but such theology is dangerous and negligent, like the medical malpractice of risking the life of a patient for the sake of making him feel better for the moment. As the Lord said to Ezekiel: "If I say to the wicked man, You shall surely die; and you do not warn him or speak out to dissuade him from his wicked conduct so that he may live: that wicked man shall die for his sin, but I will hold you responsible for his death" (Ez 3, 18).

Confirmation

In the Sacrament of Confirmation, a person is sealed with the Holy Spirit. The matter of this sacrament is oil; for in the Old Testament oil was a sign of blessing (wealth), strength (Christ exhorted us to rub oil on our face when fasting in order to appear strong, rather than weak through fasting), and a sign of joy. Kings would be anointed with oil, and the very word "Christos" (Messiah) means "anointed one". All the personal gifts of the Holy Spirit, as well as the virtues of faith, hope, and charity are strengthened in the Sacrament of Confirmation. We are given a more profound sharing in the threefold identity of Christ, for we are anointed

34

priest, **prophet**, and **king**. The oil of Confirmation is chrism oil, and it contains some aromatic substance that is blessed by the bishop on Holy Thursday. This aromatic substance quickly spreads its fragrance, symbolizing the way goodness and holiness "spreads" and influences others.

Confirmation imparts the grace to fulfill certain obligations that belong to this new state of life established by this sacrament; a confirmed teenager has a tremendous responsibility. He or she is anointed priest (not to be confused with the ministerial priesthood), and a priest is one who offers sacrifice. The confirmed teenager is called to offer his life in sacrifice, to live no longer for himself, but for Christ and his kingdom. He or she is anointed prophet, and so he or she is called to proclaim the good news of eternal life first and foremost through the witness of his/her life. By living for truth, he/she is witnessing to the truth. And finally, he/she is anointed king. A king is one who governs and one who serves. The grace of Confirmation enables us to more readily order the various elements of the self, such as the complex network of human emotions, in accordance with the demands of reason in order to more readily serve Christ.

Eucharist

Love desires to give itself. We see this especially in the love between husband and wife who give themselves to one another bodily. That is why Christ offers us his entire self (body, blood, soul and divinity) in the Eucharist.

But a person who will not eat will soon die. The same law applies in the spiritual realm. A person who cuts himself off from the Eucharist is one who will eventually die spiritually, and one who feeds on the

Eucharist periodically will suffer from a kind of spiritual malnutrition.

A friend of mine was studying theology in Nebraska one summer when he was approached by a former Satanist. She made the comment that Catholics are largely unaware of the tremendous power that is available in the Eucharist. She informed him that a true Satanist can tell the difference between a consecrated host and one that is not consecrated (one that is merely a wafer of bread). For the Eucharist is literally Christ's body. I am always astounded at the number of Catholics who typically regard the Eucharist as merely a symbol of the body of Christ. They do so not because they refuse to believe Catholic teaching, but rather because they have never heard otherwise—or if they have, never gave it much thought.

A priest is one who is given the power to change the substance of ordinary bread and wine into the substance of Christ's body and blood. This is traditionally known as **transubstantiation**. Ordinary things or beings exist primarily as substances (water, gold, iron, oak tree, etc), but there are secondary modes of being that *exist in* substances (such as color, size, place, time, etc.). These secondary modes of being are called accidents (from the Latin: *ac-cidere* - to fall upon). Their mode of being is to "inhere in" things; they do not exist independently, as substances do. A substance exists *per se* (through itself), while accidents, such as quantity, quality, where, when, etc., depend upon substance in order to be, but substance does not depend upon accidents in order to be (but only in order to be known). The first accident of a material substance is quantity (extension into parts outside of parts). Following upon quantity is the accident of quality, which is further divided into affective qualities (color, taste, smell, etc.), figure and form, habit and disposition, and finally abilities and debilities.

The substance is not the same as its extension and qualities. These inhere in the substance; for these can change while the substance remains the same, as is the case with all accidental change. But what happens during the consecration is the complete reverse. It is the substance that changes, while the accidents remain the same. Such a change is logically possible because substance is really distinct from accident. Whether or not it actually occurs depends upon whether God chooses to work the miracle. We believe that He does; for we believe that Jesus is the eternal Person of the Word (Son), and he spoke: "Take this all of you and eat it: this is my body which will be given up for you ... this is the cup of my blood, [which] ... will be shed for you ..." In John we read:

I am the living bread that came down from heaven; whoever eats this bread will live forever; and the bread that I will give is my flesh for the life of the world....Amen, amen, I say to you, unless you eat the flesh of the Son of Man and drink his blood, you do not have life within you. Whoever eats my flesh and drinks my blood has eternal life, and I will raise him on the last day. For my flesh is true food, and my blood is true drink. Whoever eats my flesh and drinks my blood remains in me and I in him. (Jn 6, 51-56)

The Church has always believed that what we receive in the Eucharist is the real body, blood, soul and divinity of Jesus Christ. Very early on, around the year 150 AD (about 60 years after the gospel of John was written), Justin Martyr wrote:

This food we call Eucharist, of which no one is allowed to partake except one who believes that the things we teach are true,...For we do not receive these things as common bread or common drink; but as Jesus

Christ our Saviour being incarnate by God's word took flesh and blood for our salvation, so also we have been taught that the food consecrated by the word of prayer which comes from him, from which our flesh and blood are nourished by transformation, is the flesh and blood of the incarnate Jesus.[7]

But not only do we receive the substance of Christ's body under the appearance of bread, and the substance of his blood under the appearance of wine. What we receive is his body "given up for you", his blood "shed for you." It is his body in the act of self-giving, in his perfect act of self-sacrifice. It is the sacrifice of Calvary, the perfect act of religion made on behalf of the entire human race that we receive literally into ourselves. In the Eucharist, we are joined to Christ's perfect act of religion. We become that act. The Mass is a sacrifice, the one sacrifice of the cross made present, that is, re-presented at each moment when and where it is celebrated validly. This is the miracle of the Mass, namely that the one, historical, unrepeatable sacrifice of Calvary can be made present on the altar throughout history, such that anyone present at an ordinary Mass is in reality just as present at the foot of the cross as Mary and John were two thousand years ago. There is literally nothing greater that we can do than to attend an ordinary Mass, especially on a daily basis; happy indeed are those who have the faith to believe this.

Aboriginal Myth and the Sacrifice of the Mass

There are myriads of creation myths of the aboriginal peoples around the world, from Australia to Africa, to North America and the Amazon basin. For the aborigines, religion is life itself. Life is an emulation of the gods of their myths. Everything they do, whether that is hunting, cooking, giving birth, or making things of various sorts, it is all sacred to the degree that it imitates the acts of the gods or ancestors whose deeds are beautifully recounted in their myths and legends.

The aborigines believe that the great sky god created lesser deities, who in turn created the earth, mountains, rock formations, trees, rivers, etc., and man—not to mention his living patterns. But all this took place in what is referred to as the creation period (the dreaming), a period of time that is sacred, for it is a time that measures the very work of the gods. This sacred time is of a different dimension than ordinary time.

To get a better understanding of this, consider the *Chronicles of Narnia*, by C. S. Lewis, for example, *The Lion, the Witch and the Wardrobe*. When the children pass through the wardrobe, they enter a different world, the world of Narnia, and many years in Narnia amount to about a minute or two of earth time.

Similarly, for aboriginal man, there is earth time (profane time), and sacred time in which the gods dwell, and the two are not parallel, but ritual is the means by which sacred time is brought into contact with profane time. In performing ritual, such as an elaborate initiation ritual—which may require an entire season to complete—, they imitate the ancestors or lesser deities, and in doing so, sacred time is made contemporary with profane time. The two different realms are in contact, all as a result of ritual. In other words, the acts of the gods are made present, in the here and now, through the ritual acts of the aborigines, and it is by virtue of this contact that primal man is renewed, strengthened, and made holy.

There is one feature of their myths and legends, however, that I have always found particularly striking, and this feature is found all over the world, in the myths of the Australian, African, South and North American tribes. In their myths, there is very often an account of a murdered god. It is an unjust murder of an innocent

deity or ancestor, and from the body of this murdered
deity will come vegetation of all kinds, i.e., beans,
melons, corn, tobacco, or a certain tree from whose
wood are made flutes that produce enchanting sounds,
like the archetypal flute that was played by the murdered
god in sacred time. To create such a flute out of the
wood of this particular tree was a ritual that makes
present the murdered deity. And to harvest the crops in
the fall is a ritual act that includes sacrificial offering to
the deity and festivities, since it is from his sacrificed
body that the fruits of the earth come to us year after
year.

Even the head hunting and cannibalism of certain
tribes can only be understood in light of their myths, and
it is always an offering to the murdered god, a re-
enactment of the myth, for the sake of the blessings that
will inevitably follow upon such ritual.

What is it in the human subconscious that can
account for this universal theme found in the creation
myths and legends of tribes separated by oceans and
thousands of miles?

How do we account for Genesis, chapter 14, 18-20,
in which the ancient king of Salem and "priest of God
the Most High", Melchizedek, brings bread and wine to
Abraham, with a blessing? Melchizedek, a pre-Israelite,
prefigures the priesthood that Christ established, and of
course Melchizedek knew nothing about this
foreshadowing or prefiguring, nor did Abraham.

And well after Abraham, at the time of the Exodus,
the Passover feast was established. The Seder plate
prefigures the Eucharist as well. Here the original
Passover lamb is sacrificed, and it is the blood that
marks the doorposts of the Israelites that is the promise
of their freedom. To share in the Seder meal is to be part
of that Exodus.

For the Jews, to share a meal is to enter into
communion with all who are at the table, because all

share in the one food, which is a source of life. When they celebrate the Passover, they believe that what is past is made present in the here and now, and so each time the Passover is celebrated throughout the centuries, Moses is present in their midst; Jews who celebrate Passover believe they leave Egypt with all of Israel at the time of the Exodus.

The gospel account of the miracle of the multiplication of the loaves and fish also prefigures the coming reality of the Eucharist.

We see this prefiguring of the Eucharist not only in the New Testament, and not only in the history of Israel, which includes a small account of the pagan king Melchizedek, but it goes back further, as far back as aboriginal man.

God leaves clues all throughout history, in every continent and in every people, clues about where He can be found. In the Person of Christ, myth becomes reality. All that the aborigines dreamt of, believed and articulated is affirmed by God and is brought to reality. We worship a murdered God, a crucified God, and from his body come the "fruit of the vine and the work of human hands", the bread of life and the cup of salvation. To partake of this thanksgiving sacrifice is to enter into him, to live in him. And just as aboriginal man saw ritual as the way of making sacred time contemporary with ordinary time, a way of making it touch profane time thereby renewing it, so too has this come to reality in the Eucharist, because to be present at an ordinary Mass, like this one, is to be just as present at the foot of the cross as Mary and John were two thousand years ago. The sacrifice of Good Friday, which took place 2000 years ago, is made contemporary, that is, re-presented in the here and now. It is not this or that priest who is offering the sacrifice, it is Christ who is the priest and who offers the sacrifice, and Christ is the victim, the murdered God, who is being offered. The individual priest is only acting in the Person of Christ (*in persona Christi*).

And we believe that Christ is the new Passover lamb, whose blood frees us from the slavery of sin and death, and of whose flesh we partake, making us one with that sacrificial offering.

And so to eat of this Eucharist is to become one not only with every member of Christ's mystical body, past and present, but it is to become intimately one with all the faithful of Israel, as well as Primal religious man, the aborigines, who knew something of this sacrifice, however obscure that understanding might have been.

When I was explaining to some students that the Eucharist is truly the body and blood of Christ, not merely a symbol of his body and blood, one girl raised her hand and said: "It can't be. That would make us cannibals". And of course she had no idea of the religious significance of ancient tribal cannibalism; she saw primitive man with the condescending eyes of the Western world, that is, as backward and unintelligent. But it is not that we cannot be like them; rather, when you understand the significance of their myths and rituals, we begin to see that we can be, we are, and they are like us. They yearned to participate in the life of the gods, that is, they yearned for the sacred to repeatedly touch their profane existence and make it holy and complete, as we do now.

God answers man's deepest aspirations in the Incarnation, and ultimately in the Eucharist. There is nothing we can do that is holier than to center our life around the Eucharist. We need to burn with a desire for the Eucharist, to hunger for the Eucharist, and we need to pray more often before the Blessed Sacrament. St. John Bosco used to tell his young people that if you wish to see miracles in your life, pray often before the Blessed Sacrament. God is so merciful and humble that He joined a human nature, entered into human suffering, and died on a cross. Cleary He loves to play hide and seek, and like a good player He hides Himself in unexpected places, under a humble disguise. He continues to hide in our midst under the ordinary and humble appearance of a wafer of bread. After consecration, it is no longer bread, although it looks like bread, tastes and feels like bread. It is the substance of his murdered and resurrected body.

Reconciliation

As was said earlier, the Church is Christ's Mystical Body. Now a body is a unity. In other words, the parts of the body are not isolated units unto themselves; rather, they are parts *of the whole*, and they exist to serve and maintain the integrity of the whole. When a part of the body is injured, such as a stubbed toe, it is the one whole organism that feels the pain; the one person has been injured. All injury is, strictly speaking, injury of a part or parts. But we do not say that the part has been injured, but that the person has been injured. If we speak of the part as injured, it is always in relation to the whole, i.e., "my toe", or "I hurt my toe". So too for Christ's Mystical Body, the Church. All members of the Church are members of a living body. Sin affects the entire body, just as an injured part affects the entire organism. That is why sin is a public affair, and never a private matter between God and the sinner. If sin only affected one's relationship with God, then perhaps a person could make a case against the need to confess to a priest. But the priest represents the Church, and absolution (release) is forgiveness in the name of Christ's Mystical Body:

"And when he had said this, he breathed on them and said to them, 'Receive the Holy Spirit. Whose sins you forgive are forgiven them, and whose sins you retain are retained" (Jn 20, 22).

For if my sin affects every member of Christ's body, then I must seek reconciliation to the Church as well as to God; I must seek forgiveness from every member of the Church. But this is not possible. That is why the priest acts in the name of the Church in absolving a person from sin. In being reconciled to Christ's body, I am reconciled to Christ, and in being reconciled to Christ, I am reconciled to God. The graces received in the sacrament of reconciliation strengthen us to eventually overcome the sins that we currently struggle with.

Interestingly enough, there is one sin that cannot be forgiven, namely, blasphemy of the Holy Spirit:

"Therefore, I say to you, every sin and blasphemy will be forgiven, but blasphemy against the Spirit will not be forgiven. And whoever speaks a word against the Son of Man will be forgiven; but whoever speaks against the Holy Spirit will not be forgiven, either in this age or in the age to come" (Mt 12, 31-32).

This has always been a source of wonder for theologians throughout the ages. According to Catholic theological tradition, there are six ways to blaspheme the Holy Spirit. These are **despair, presumption, final impenitence, obstinacy, resisting the known truth**, and finally **envy of another's spiritual good**.

To sin against the Holy Spirit is to take pleasure in the malice of sin for its own sake. The reason that such a sin cannot be forgiven is that the Holy Spirit is the source of the remission of sins, and the six ways of blaspheming the Holy Spirit are sins that are directly contrary to the remission of sins. For there are certain effects of the Holy Spirit that work to prevent the choosing of evil, such as the theological virtue of hope, the gift of fear, openness to truth, a healthy sense of shame, delight in the good fortune and blessings of another, etc. Blasphemy of the Holy Spirit results from a special contempt of one or more of these effects.

First, consider **despair**. I once taught a student who chose not to receive the sacrament of Reconciliation when the opportunity arose during a week in Lent. There is nothing terribly unusual about this. But I decided to ask him why he chose not to take advantage of the opportunity. It was his reply that was somewhat distressing. He said that there is no way that God would forgive him for what he had done. I tried to argue with him, but he kept insisting that God could not possibly forgive him his sin. He wouldn't tell me what his sin was, but I spent a great deal of time trying to convince him that there is nothing we can do that God will not forgive, as long as we approach him with contrition (sorrow for sin) and ask for forgiveness. He finally decided to receive the sacrament.

Now, this was not an instance of the despair that is blasphemy of the Holy Spirit, because he was forgiven of his sins. This was a case of unbelief. After listening to some basic truths of the gospel, he chose to believe (faith) and to hope, and so he cooperated with divine grace, which was moving him to repentance. But the despair that is an instance of blasphemy of the Holy Spirit is similar. The difference is that the person has contempt for the mercy of God—most probably because he has never shown mercy to another in his life—and so he persists in his despair of the divine mercy. Such a person will not seek forgiveness with a contrite heart, because he chooses to believe that his sin is too great for God to forgive. Hence, he will not receive it, for the conditions of the remission of sins are contrition and the asking of forgiveness.

We must always remember that our sins are never too great for God to forgive. Fear of this despair is the reason why we say, at the end of the Hail Mary: "…pray for us sinners, now and at the hour of our death". According to some of the great saints and doctors of the Church, our final hour will be the most difficult hour of our lives; for it is at this hour that the forces of hell will be unleashed against us, bringing to our awareness all the sins that we have committed throughout our lifetime, in order to induce us to finally despair of the mercy of God. Prudent indeed it is to beseech the Blessed Mother to intercede for us during this final and most difficult hour.

Presumption is the opposite of despair. Many years ago when teaching in a rather difficult area of Toronto, I would often engage in conversation students who were regular drug dealers. I don't believe it is possible to reason with a drug dealer. They operate on a very low level of "conscience", and so if one is going to have any success in getting a drug dealer to change his ways, one has to be willing to sound like a fundamentalist preacher. And so I would talk to them about hell and eternal punishment in a way that would frighten any other person of normal conscience. And what I discovered in the course of my conversations with these kids is that they were convinced that they would be forgiven for all their sins, because "God forgives all sins". These kids had total contempt for the law of God, and they had no fear of God, because somehow they got it into their heads that God was some giant "doormat" in the sky who automatically forgave all sins, without any requirements on the part of the sinner. Such people will not seek God's forgiveness, because they "presume" that they already have it, despite their criminal lifestyle. To die in such a state of contempt for the divine justice is to die condemned.

When we consider the inordinateness and shamefulness of our sins, we are aroused to repentance. But impenitence resists this grace. It is **final impenitence** that is a sin against the remission of sins. A priest friend of mine was called to a scene in which a university student jumped off a building, breaking her back and probably almost every other bone in her body. It was clear from her style of dress and the words she was uttering that her suicide was part of a satanic rite of some kind. She was not going to live, and so he asked her, as part of the anointing rite, if she was sorry for all her sins. Her reply was a sardonic laughter. She spent her final minute mocking the priest and everything he had to offer.

The lure of sin is very deceptive; it is nothing but an empty promise. There is no benefit that comes from sin that cannot be had through virtue, along with so much more. In fact, whatever goods we sacrifice in this life for the sake of the kingdom of God will be possessed in their perfect goodness when we possess the Supreme Good in heaven. A consideration of the very small benefit that is sought in sinful acts tends to prevent the will from being hardened in sin, but this consideration is removed by **obstinacy**, whereby a person hardens his purpose by clinging to sin.

If a person loves sin for its own sake, he will hate truth, for the truth will always witness against him. **Resistance of the known truth** is a freely chosen posture that prevents a person from allowing the work of the Holy Spirit to be accomplished within him. This posture is far more widespread than we might tend to imagine at first. Recall the question Pontius Pilate addressed to Jesus: "What is truth?" (Jn 18, 38). The Truth was standing directly in front of him, and it was this Truth that he chose to crucify. Pilate's skepticism has become the cultural norm in the Western world; hence, the current popularity of Deconstructionism, which denies that there is any such thing as a universal or absolute truth. Deconstructionism embraces a kind of Perspectivism that maintains that all we have in the world are myriads of perspectives, and that something is true only within the relative framework of a particular point of view. Such perspectives are merely human constructs, built up in order to make sense of a world intrinsically absurd and unintelligible. Ultimately, truth is a fiction. Such a philosophical standpoint leaves us free to adopt any perspective we desire, in particular the one that allows us to continue in the lifestyle of our choice, regardless of how sinful that lifestyle might appear to a particular longstanding religious tradition.

Every person has sufficient grace to avoid sin in his life. Whenever we experience the impetus of divine grace within us, for example, the desire to pray, or to attend Mass on a regular basis, to fast, or to perform some act of charity, etc., it is very important that we not neglect it so as to render it sterile, but cooperate with it and allow the grace to come to fruition. Sometimes it is just sloth that renders these graces sterile. But the assistance of inward grace can also be rejected through **envy of another's spiritual good**. This is difficult to explain, but envy is a desire that a person be deprived of the good that is his. It is followed by a secret delight at another's misfortune. Now, in order to grow in the grace of God, we need the help of others. Their special charisms exist for the building up of the Body of Christ, the Church. If we envy their spiritual good by virtue of inordinate self-love, we will inevitably reject their help and the benefits that accrue to us through their charisms. God offers us great gifts, but always through the instrumentality of sinful and unworthy human beings. Envy closes the doors on these gifts. We must learn to get past the obnoxious and annoying traits of human beings in order to benefit from their blessings and charisms. If we don't, we annihilate the grace that moves us forward and carries us to greater heights.

Why a person chooses to fix himself against the very source of the remission of sins is mysterious, but the decision to do so, we can be assured, is entirely free, for it is impossible to choose (and persist in that choice) a course of action that eternally determines one's fate on the basis of a decision that was not enlightened and deliberate, that is, entirely free. Genuinely free-choices present a certain impenetrable darkness to the human mind because they are self-caused, as opposed to being caused by something outside the choosing subject. But we can at least be certain that God "wills everyone to be saved and to come to the knowledge of the truth" (1 Tim 2, 4). Hence, we can be sure that each person is given sufficient grace to become a vessel in the hands of the potter. Free-choice is the ability of the vessel to choose to crumble under the potter's touch in order to be something other than what He intends it to be.

Anointing of the Sick

Sickness and death are part of the fallen human condition. The kind of death that awaits all of us—or more accurately, that comes for us all—is a result of that mysterious wound called Original Sin. We experience death as a descent into something dark and unknown. It is the breakdown and disintegration of the human person, manifesting to us the deepest truth about ourselves, namely, that ultimately we have no power: "You are dust, and to dust you shall return" (Gn 3, 19). That is one reason why death is so necessary in a fallen world. Human beings are dull of mind and slow to learn; very few of us will learn this profound lesson on the truth of our total indigence prior to death's coming, and only those who have hardened themselves into the worst enemies of truth will undergo death without learning its most important lesson.

Death in itself is anything but a happy state, and yet St. Joseph is the patron saint of a happy death. "How can death be happy?" asked one of my students. This is not easy to explain, but we may be able to get a glimpse of what it means to die happy by focusing on its preliminary, namely sickness. There is a real difference between spiritual/psychological suffering and physical suffering. The worst suffering is, without a doubt, spiritual suffering. Depression, loneliness, or the pangs of guilt, paranoia, for example, are far more difficult to live with than a body wracked with the pain of cancer or some other physical illness. A person can undergo the worst physical pain and at the same time experience, deep within himself, a profound peace, a fullness, a radiating warmth. Certainly there is no separation between soul and body, but there is a distinction. That is why the very idea of a happy death is not unthinkable.

In joining Himself to a human nature, the Second Person of the Trinity joined Himself to every human person; in other words, he entered into the depths of human suffering. Jesus tasted darkness and human pain, that is to say, God the Son, who is eternal, entered our darkness. And so it is true that in the very depths of our own personal suffering, someone is there. We never suffer alone, even though it may seem like we do. In the midst of suffering, we can find, if we are open and looking, the eternal Person of the Son, who can illuminate our darkness. In fact, to find Him there is already to be illumined. All the saints have found Him there. That is why stories of saints who have embraced suffering, who were not afraid of it, or accounts of some who have actually willed it, are not instances of neurotic perversions. Rather, they can only be understood in light of this theological implication of the Incarnation.

The sacrament of the Anointing of the Sick strengthens us and enables us to discover Christ in the midst of sickness and dying. It allows us to more readily join our sufferings to the suffering of Christ. Oil is the matter of this sacrament, and oil, as we have seen, is a natural sign of joy, blessing and strength. It is through this anointing that we are given the grace that will enable us to bear our sufferings bravely and even joyfully, and we are given the grace that will strengthen and console us in the face of death, and finally, it grants us the forgiveness of sins.

Holy Orders

Holy Orders is the sacrament through which men are given the power to carry out the sacred duties of deacons, priests, or bishops. It is the bishop who has the fullness of Orders (the fullness of the priesthood), and a priest has a sharing in the ordination of the bishop. A priest acts in the bishop's name, whereas a bishop acts in his own name, as a successor of the Apostles. A priest does not have the fullness of Orders; he cannot ordain anyone to the priesthood. So a priest is really a servant of his bishop. Those priests who act in their own name have lost a sense of what their priesthood really is in relation to their bishop.

When a man is ordained to the priesthood, he is given the power to transubstantiate, that is, to change ordinary bread and wine into Christ's body and blood. A priest is one who offers the Sacrifice of the Mass. As we said earlier, the Mass is the sacrifice of the cross made present in the "here and now", whenever and wherever Mass is celebrated validly. On Calvary, the priest and the victim were identical: Christ was the priest who offered the sacrifice to the Father, and Christ was the victim (the Lamb of God) who was offered. If this is true, and if it is true that the Mass is the same sacrifice of Calvary, then it follows that the priest does not act in the place of Christ, but rather *in persona Christi*, that is, "in the person of Christ". In other words, when you and I attend an ordinary Mass, it is not the priest whose name you know who is offering the sacrifice, but Christ who offers the sacrifice; and the victim that he offers is himself (Christ).

Why Women Are Not Ordained

I don't recall his source, but Thomist scholar Dr. F. F. Centore used to point out to us that according to Aquinas, women make better saints than men. And back in the early 80s, I recall reading Butler's Lives of the Saints and being struck by just how much female saints outnumber male saints; I believe it is by about two thirds. And one cannot read the Latin Fathers for a reasonable stretch without coming across the notion that the Church is a woman. She is the bride of Christ and the Mother of Christians. As St. Augustine comments on the wedding at Cana: "The Lord, on being invited, came to the marriage. What wonder if He came to that house to a marriage, having come into this world to a marriage? For, indeed, if He came not to a marriage, He has not here a bride".8

The more a person is familiar with the fundamentals of Catholic theology, the more obvious it is that if priesthood had primarily to do with the talents and gifts of individual persons, women would be priests. To lead a school in the capacity of a principal or to assume public office has everything to do with the abilities, the talents, and the gifts of the individual person aspiring towards such positions (such as court judge or Member of Parliament). That is why there are female principals, judges, and political leaders, many of whom are superior to many of their male counterparts. And who would doubt that there are women who could in all likelihood preach a far more inspiring homily than does the average male priest today, or offer more practical and prudent counseling to couples going through marital difficulties? Why then are there not women priests?

The obvious answer is that priesthood does not primarily have to do with the talents and gifts of the individual priest. If a priest does not know that at the time of his ordination, he will learn that difficult truth shortly thereafter. If he refuses to take in the lesson, his days as a priest are probably numbered, that is, he will probably end up leaving the priesthood. For his priesthood has nothing to do with him.

Priesthood is the second greatest gift that every priest has received. Like his first greatest gift, namely faith, it is sheer gift, gratuitously given without having earned it or deserved it in the slightest. It is all about Christ, not about him. Christ is priest, and a priest is one who offers sacrifice. What is unique about Christ's priesthood is that he is both priest and victim, and the meaning of the ministerial priesthood is entirely concentrated in the priesthood of Christ, which in turn is concentrated upon his offering of himself on Calvary. It all goes back to Good Friday.

Every sacrament is a composite of both sign and word. Every sign that is sublimated by the sacrament already has a natural sign value. For example, the natural sign used in Baptism is water. The reason is that water is a natural sign of purity, cleansing, life, and death. We use water to clean ourselves and other things, and living things need water in order to survive and grow, and too much water kills; it is the most powerful and destructive force in nature. Water is thus the most apt sign to signify the imparting of the supernatural life of grace, supernatural cleansing and purification, and a spiritual dying to the old Adam and a rising in Christ. The words that render Baptism a valid sacrament are, "I baptize you in the name of the Father, and of the Son,

and of the Holy Spirit." Should a person have been
baptized with milk, or vegetable oil, etc., the baptism
would be considered invalid. This is not because milk
and vegetable oil are inferior substances. Rather, they
are not natural signs of cleansing, life and death. Milk
naturally signifies nourishment, and oil naturally signifies
wealth and strength. In fact, that is precisely why oil is
the natural sign used in the sacrament of Confirmation,
which is a confirming or strengthening of the graces
received in Baptism. If a bishop were to anoint a child
with acrylic paint, the sacrament would not be imparted.

The natural signs used in the Sacrament of the
Eucharist are bread and wine, because these two
substances have a universal significance. Visit any liquor
store and the international division of the layout strikes
one immediately: Italian, French, California, Ontario,
etc. Every culture also has its bread: Italian, French,
Portuguese, German, Middle East, etc. In other words,
bread and wine are universal signs of nourishment. And
the Church is '*katholikos*' (kata-holos) or universal, that
is, of all nations. The New Covenant is an International
Covenant, not a national one as was the Old Covenant.
That is why the sacrament of the new covenant, the
Eucharist, must employ signs that have an international
significance, because the Eucharist is the food that
sustains the universal Church and spiritually nourishes
every believer who receives it. The reason this is so is
that the Eucharist is no longer bread and wine. It is the
substance of Christ's body and blood.

When the priest pronounces the words: "This is my
body", at that point the substance of bread changes into
the substance of Christ's body, while the accidents of the
bread (quantity, place, posture, and its affective qualities
such as color, taste, odor, etc.,) remain the same. When
he says: "This is my blood", at that very instant the
substance of wine changes into the substance of Christ's
blood, while the accidents of the wine (quantity, place,

posture, and its affective qualities such as color, taste, odor, etc.,) remain the same. That is why it looks like bread and tastes like bread. But the substance is something else entirely; for substance is really distinct from its accidents (attributes), which regularly change while the substance remains the same. Thus, as was said above, it is logically possible for God to reverse the order if He so chooses, and Catholics believe that God works the miracle of transubstantiation every time Mass is said, by changing the substances, but leaving their accidental modes of being intact.

But if we pay attention to the words of consecration, we notice that there is more to this than what we've covered so far: "Take this, all of you, and eat of it, for this is my body, which will be given up for you...Take this all of you and drink from it, for this is the chalice of my blood...which will be poured out for you and for many for the forgiveness of sins." The words of consecration are sacrificial. We receive the body of Christ that was *given up for us* two thousand years ago and the blood that was *poured out for us* at the same time. Christ was only sacrificed once, but the body that we are given is the same body that was given up for us on Good Friday. That sacrifice is mysteriously and miraculously perpetuated throughout history wherever Mass is said, and so it is no exaggeration to say that to be present at an ordinary Mass is to be just as present at the foot of the cross as Mary and John were two thousand years ago. That is what is meant by the expression "the sacrifice of the Mass".

So what does this have to do with the ordination of women? A woman is a sign of creation and of the Church redeemed. A man is not. He cannot conceive new life within himself, nurture it for nine months and give birth to it. The Church is both bride and mother. Christ is bridegroom: "But the time will come when the bridegroom is taken away from them, and then they will fast" (Mt 9, 16). The Church receives his word, his baptism, and his blood, and she generates sons and daughters of God in Baptism as a result of her union with him. But it was the bridegroom who gave himself up for his bride, the Church: "Men may offer to a bride every sort of earthly ornament, gold, silver, precious stones, houses, slaves, estates, farms, —but will any give his own blood?"[9]

The image of a woman saying Mass obscures the fundamental symbolism of the priesthood; just as using wine to baptize a child would obscure what is taking place sacramentally in baptism. For the Mass is the sacrifice of Calvary re-presented in the here and now. The priest is acting not in his own person (*in persona propria*), but *in persona Christi*. Christ is the priest making the offering and the victim being offered, because the Mass is the sacrifice of the cross. *It was not the Church, the bride of Christ, who gave herself up for him.* But that is precisely what is being said if a woman, a sign of creation redeemed, were to take bread in her hands saying: "Take this all of you and eat of it, this is my body which will be given up for you".

That is why the Church maintains that she has no power to validly ordain women any more than she has the power to baptize a child with wine or oil, or validly anoint a person with acrylic paint or holy water. It has nothing to do with grades of perfection or an alleged superiority of men over women. It has everything to do with the sacramental symbolism of the priesthood.

Those who have little difficulty with this are the ones who seem to have an appreciation for the importance and central place of symbol and ritual in the development, expression and communication of a culture.

Matrimony

Matrimony is the sacrament through which a baptized man and a baptized woman join themselves in a one flesh union until death severs it. As a sacrament, it is a source of divine grace that enables them to be loving and faithful spouses to one another and good parents to their children. We've already called attention to the fact that Christ is the bridegroom and the Church is his Bride. As such, marriage is a sign of the love that Christ has for his Bride, the Church. One cannot naturally love one's spouse as Christ has loved the Church; we must be given the grace to do so. Matrimony channels the grace to love with a supernatural charity. Christ said that "The Son of Man did not come to be served but to serve..." (Mt 20, 28). And so if men have a duty to love their wives as Christ loves the Church (Eph 5, 25), then it is the role of the man not to be served by his wife, but to serve his wife throughout his married life.

Because marriage is a joining of male and female into one body, marriage is essentially a community of love and life—for life is generated as a result of the physical union of husband and wife. Love is essentially unitive; it tends to a union of some degree (i.e., a handshake, hug, kiss, etc.). But genuine love is also effusive. It inevitably seeks to communicate goodness to another, to have another (the beloved) participate in the goodness that the lover enjoys. The love between husband and wife, if genuine and not selfish, will tend to love another human being into existence; for the couple will desire to communicate the goodness of their relationship to another human being, and this child will be the fruit of that love and a living witness and expression of their one flesh union.

All marriages that take place in the Church are presumed valid, unless proven otherwise; but why are some marriages annulled? There are various impediments that render a marriage invalid. The most obvious impediment is **coercion**. The consent to marry

must be freely given, and so coercing a person to marry
another cannot result in a valid marriage.

Psychological immaturity is also an impediment.
Some couples simply have no idea what marriage entails
and do not have the strength of character to make the
commitment that marriage requires. Having a previous
marriage that is not annulled is probably the most
frequent impediment today. Another impediment which
also violates the requirement of free consent is
sometimes called **fraud**. The person you end up
marrying may turn out to be someone entirely different
than the person you thought you married; he or she may
have kept hidden certain aspects of themselves that, had
you known about, would have changed your decision to
marry him/her.

The **deliberate intention not to have children**
renders a marriage invalid. This is not the same as
infertility (the inability to conceive a child). It refers to a
decision to close one's marriage to new life. It is an act
of the will. This renders a marriage invalid because
marriage begins with the intention to become one body.
To intend not to conceive is to intend that sperm and
egg never meet. Such a couple does not will a complete
one flesh union. In other words, they do not intend to
marry in as much as marriage is a joining of two into one
body. Finally, in order for a marriage to be valid, the
couple must intend a permanent and exclusive union,
and so a couple that leaves an opening for divorce do
not establish a valid marriage.

A Note on Non-Christian Religions

Many students wonder where the great religions of
the world fit into this theological scheme of things. This
is not an easy topic to deal with, and when doing so we
tread upon very murky territory. There are very few cut

and dried answers here. But I would like to call attention to a few points.

First, if Jesus is who he claims to be, then it follows irrefutably that he is everything that every religion is looking for. What exactly does this mean? This is where we have to be careful. Does it mean that non-Christian religions are false? No, it does not.

When carefully studying the religions of the world, we notice that one religion in particular stands out from all the others, and this is the religion of Judaism. In Judaism, God takes the initiative and reveals Himself to Abraham. The other great religions do not claim to be anything more than man's word about God. It is true that Islam claims that the Koran was given to Muhammad by the angel Gabriel, but the content of the Koran does not require an act of faith as such, that is, an assent of the mind to truths that transcend the grasp of human reason. The content is accessible to human reason. In this sense, Islam is the perfect natural religion. The religions of the world are packed with profoundly insightful truths about God and human nature. But the claim of Judaism is unique. Here, God establishes a covenant with Abraham and promises that his descendants will be as numerous as the stars of the sky, and that in him all nations will find blessing.

Judaism is a historical relationship, a covenant, one that was initiated by God. It is a revealed religion, and not a natural one. Christianity is rooted in Judaism, and it too claims to be a revealed religion. In fact, Christianity believes the covenant established by Christ at the Last Supper is the new covenant foretold by Jeremiah and Ezekiel: "The days are coming, says the Lord, when I will make a new covenant with the house of Israel and the house of Judah" (Jer 31, 31). No other religion makes such claims. And so we must be sure to approach these religions on their terms, and not on our terms. We need not demand from them anything more than what they claim to offer. When we adopt this approach, we allow these religions to enrich our lives and actually help us to understand our own faith better.

Consider that Jesus said: "I am the Way, the Truth, and the Life" (Jn 14, 6). Moreover, in his letter to the Colossians, Paul says that it is Christ in whom are hidden all the treasures of wisdom and knowledge (Col 2, 3). If this is true, then the more I know Christ, the more readily will I be able to discover the real truths in the religions of the world. Or, consider this from another angle. In me one does not find the fullness of the treasures of wisdom and knowledge, but only in Christ. And so there is a kind of mutual conditioning that occurs in the life of a true believer with respect to the world religions. If I love Christ, in whom are all the treasures of wisdom and knowledge, then I will love all that is true in the world religions, and I will reject nothing that is true and good. Since that fullness lies hidden in Him—not in me—then these other religions can help me to discover truths that I already have potentially, but which lie hidden in the Person of Christ, truths which I would otherwise have overlooked.

Who can deny the truth of the fundamental insights of Buddhism, for example? That the suffering of this world is caused primarily and for the most part by inordinate desire? What Christian is not impressed by the beautiful tales on almsgiving found in *The Sayings of Muhammad*, for example? What Christian cannot find tremendous food for thought and inspiration in *The Upanishads*, the *Tao Te Ching*, the *Dhammapada*, the writings of Chuang Tzu or Confucius, etc? Christ does not render these treasures superfluous. Rather, he opens us up to their true splendor, and through them we can indeed come to know ourselves better, and know Christ better; for if Christ is the Truth, then he is the source of all the truths we find in them. Thus, knowing these truths helps us to know their source more perfectly.

But if Christ is the source of grace, can a non-Christian be in a state of grace? Strictly speaking, it is not possible to know with certainty whether or not anyone in particular is in a state of grace, including ourselves. When asked if she knew she was in God's grace, St. Joan of Arc replied: "If I am not, may it please God to put me in it; if I am, may it please God to keep me there" (Cf. Acts of the trial of St. Joan of Arc). But just as truth is found among the nations, so too is grace (*Ad Gentes,* 9). For there is no doubt in my mind that the Mahatma Gandhi was a much greater man that I will ever be, and I have known many Muslim students who pray and fast faithfully every day during the month of Ramadan. How is it possible for a Muslim teenager to be so devoted to God and faithfully carry out such personal sacrifice and not be in a state of grace?

Being in the state of grace is not about having correct theology or knowing specific truths. A Muslim may respond to the movements of interior grace to a much greater degree than the lukewarm Catholic, who is so indifferent to the demands of his religion that he does not even bother to fast on Ash Wednesday and Good Friday, let alone an entire month of the year. If Christianity is the right religion, Catholics may have more cause for fear and concern, for they will have a great deal more to answer for on the Day of Judgment. If I have been given much more than Mohandas K. Gandhi, what excuse do I have for giving back to God so much less than he did? If you have been baptized, confirmed, given the theological virtues of faith, hope, and charity as well as the seven personal gifts of the Holy Spirit, the grace of regeneration, the real presence of Christ in the Eucharist, the opportunity to receive forgiveness of sins and the grace to overcome those sins in the future, strength in sickness, graces in matrimony, the revelation of the Old and New Testaments, sacramentals and the lives of the saints, how are you

61

going to render an account for the fact that your life is outwardly no different than the average Hedonist, while the Muslim student who sat next to you all year prayed five times a day facing the East, gave a rather large percentage of his income to the poor, and did not allow even a drop of water to pass between his lips during daylight hours for an entire month of the year, without even half of the resources you were given?

It seems to me that the world is centuries away from real unity and religious peace, and I believe that the two extremes of religious self-righteousness—an attitude which we tend to encounter among Christians and Muslims of the fundamentalist stripe—and Restricted Indifferentism, made popular by Rousseau, which regards all religions as on a par, each one leading to the same destination, do not serve the ends of religious peace. The former—at least with regard to Christians—fails to grasp the positive implications of the Incarnation of Truth, while the latter is a subtle denial of the claims of Judaism and Christianity. It seems to me that Catholics can only be front-runners in the movement towards religious dialogue. And this dialogue cannot be genuine if there is a relinquishing of our convictions or a watering down of the contents of faith. Genuine dialogue (*dia logos*) is a movement towards the Logos, and the Logos is the measure of what each of us has to say. *In arche erin Logon* (In the beginning was the Word). *Arche* is the foundation of the real, the source and origin of things. This is what all of the Greek natural philosophers were seeking, which is why theology can and has benefited so much from their discoveries. And so *arche* (beginning) does not mean "beginning" as in the temporal beginning of a motion. It refers rather to the beginning of a causal principle, and a cause is a principle upon which something proceeds with dependence. The reason behind everything that is, is the Word (Logos), who is with God and who is God. He became flesh and dwelt among us.

By loving and embracing this Word more intimately, we make ourselves more able to enter into genuine dialogue. The world religions are there for us, and we are there for them; our only duty is to enter into dialogue, not to direct this great conversation to an end that we have envisioned. This conversation and where it will lead is too great for us to comprehend. The Logos will govern the movement and direction of the dialogue, for everything depends upon the Logos. It is up to us to simply become a part of the current of that discussion. When we try to control it, we begin relinquishing essential tenets of our faith, and this renders dialogue impossible. We end up creating an artificial unity, which does not, will not, and cannot last.

Chapter 4: On the Seven Capital Sins and What Can Be Done About Them

St. Bernadette, in answer to the question: "What is a sinner?" said that "A sinner is one who loves evil". Her answer was clever, because she did not say "does", but "loves". We all do evil, for all of us sin; for we are frail and prone to sin and self-seeking. The goal of the spiritual life is to die completely to this inordinate love of self so as to become one with God, which is what our hearts are restless for ultimately. But not everyone "loves" sin. Those who do love darkness (Jn 3, 19) will simply refuse to enter into battle against their own tendency to sin. But if you know from within that you do not love darkness and that you want to love God more fully so as to possess Him forever in eternity, then you must choose to engage in the struggle against your own particular tendencies to sin and self-seeking.

We all have our own particular battle ground, that is, our own unique struggles. What I have found over the years is that the seven capital sins are a continuum that marks a range on which each person can begin to outline, in general terms, his own particular battle ground. This range begins with the most spiritual and serious of the capital sins and moves towards the more physical and least serious - note however that "least serious" does not mean that they are not serious. Indeed, each of the seven is capable of killing the grace of God within the soul, rendering the soul dead and thus empty of the divine life.

The first of the capital sins is **pride**, which is inordinate or disordered self-esteem. In the extreme, it is the decision to make oneself one's own god, that is, to make oneself the measure of what is true and good. Now the word "capital" comes from the Latin caput, which means 'head'. A capital sin is at the head of a host of sins that are its offspring. The sin of pride in particular spawns a number of sins, such as conceit, boasting, stubbornness, disobedience, discord, argumentativeness, competitiveness, a haughty demeanor, patronization, isolating oneself out of a sense of superiority, hypocrisy, and prevarication, that is, putting on a façade (wearing a mask). In a religious context, this means Phariseeism or clericalism.

Pride is the root of all sin, and so all of us will struggle with pride at some level; for when a person sins—regardless of the sin—he deliberately chooses to do what he knows to be contrary to God's will. In that sense, he has chosen to "be his own god". But there are some who struggle with—or take delight in—this sin to a greater degree than others. Usually, but not always, they are the very intelligent.

If we find that this is one of our struggles, we need to pray for humility. The word 'humility' is derived from the Latin *humus*, which means soil or dirt. The human person is really a pile of dirt, made living by a spiritual soul. We are "holy soil"—for human life is holy—, but we are dust and ashes nevertheless. It is matter that severely limits us—angels are unencumbered by matter, which is why they are so much more intelligent than human beings. A good remedy for pride is to meditate on our limitations, for example, on the sheer number of people in this world who in very specific ways are so much more talented than we are. There are so many gifts I do not have that others do have. Some have great mathematical minds, or historical minds, great scientific minds, or philosophical minds, technological minds, etc. There are people who can suffer more than I can, who are more generous, who are more humble, who are better looking, etc. We can also meditate on the level of our own dependency; for we depend on so many people for so many things we are helpless to deliver on our own. Pride is grounded in an illusion, and the more effort we put in to disillusioning ourselves through a concentration on our own radical limitations, the sooner we will begin to feel comfortable with the knowledge of those limits and the truth of our own dependency on others, which is the necessary condition for humility.

Envy, the next capital sin, involves willing that others be deprived of the goods and blessings that are theirs. It is rooted in a love of one's own good to the point that one wills others to be deprived of theirs, or seriously limited in their share of the good. It is accompanied by a secret delight in the misfortunes of others. Its offspring are jealousy, slander, feeling regret upon hearing good news about another or others, suspicion of another or other—which arises from an attempt to interpret another's virtue in a negative light ("Oh, they're only doing that because they want…" etc.)—, detraction, which is making known the faults of others, and gossip.

The remedy of envy is to pray for compassion or a deeper empathy for others. Most importantly, we should pray for the grace to desire, from the depths of our heart that others share in greater blessings than us. If this is painful, then we should take that as a clue that we need to continue to pray along these lines. In the *Litany of Humility*, we pray the following: "That others may be loved more than I, Jesus, grant me the grace to desire it. That others may be esteemed more than I, grant me the grace to desire it; that in the opinion of the world, others may increase and I may decrease, grant me the grace to desire it; that others may be chosen and I set aside, grant me the grace to desire it; that others may be praised and I go unnoticed, grant me the grace to desire it; that others may be preferred to me in everything, grant me the grace to desire it; that others may become holier than I, provided that I may become as holy as I should…" This last petition is a marvelous one, for it is a prayer that others have a higher place in heaven than us, which means that they will have a greater joy in eternity than us. To delight in retributive justice, however, is not contrary to envy; rather, justice is a good, and to want justice for a criminal is a virtue, while indifference to justice, or leniency, is a vice.

But all of us must be content with the place that God gives us, however insignificant, because God has a providential plan, and our small place within that plan is necessary in His overall scheme of things. As any mechanic knows, if a small and apparently insignificant part is not in its proper place, the whole cannot function well. To accept our limited place in the world is to love His providential plan without even understanding all its details. The greater one's acceptance of one's place, the greater is one's love for that providential plan, and holiness is found precisely in this love of God and His providence. One might have the lowest place on the "totem pole" but have a greater love of God's providence than the one occupying the highest place; it is this love that makes the former greater than the latter.

Avarice is the inordinate love of possessing. Among other things, it is rooted in a lack of faith that God is in control, that is, a lack of faith in divine providence. One fails to find one's security in God and so one develops a disordered desire for security and whatever can procure it. Avarice is fundamentally an inordinate love of the goods of this world. Its offspring are anxiety, stress, hardness of heart (i.e., towards the needs of others), indifference to the suffering and poverty of others, deceit, fraud, violence, and often loneliness.

The remedy for avarice is to cultivate generosity. Almsgiving goes a long way in overcoming this attachment to money and property. There is great joy in simplifying one's life and freeing oneself from the slavery of wealth and the worries it brings. Once a person has acquired this freedom, he is free to take flight into the greater joys of the spiritual life, joys that are interior and are discovered when one begins to enter into the many rooms of the interior castle of the soul through prayer, rooms that lead to the very center wherein one finds a delight and peace with which no pleasure on earth can compare; for at the center one finds God Himself.

Anger is a capital sin that should be distinguished from what is traditionally called "righteous indignation". It is a mark of excellence that one becomes angry at the sight of injustice. The sin of anger, on the contrary, is the deliberate decision to nurse anger against another, to keep the flame alive, to refuse to let go of a grudge. The offspring of anger include revenge, unforgiveness, passive aggressive behavior, verbal abuse, cursing, rebellion, disrespect, and resentment.

The remedy for anger is forgiveness from the heart. Of course, that's easier said than done; we may need the help of a counselor to take us through the steps leading to forgiveness; nonetheless, since anger is a kind of spiritual cancer that can bring on physical disease (i.e., colitis, intestinal disease, colon and liver cancer, etc.), it is urgent to begin, as soon as possible, the difficult work of forgiving those in our lives whom we need to forgive. Most importantly, Christ has said that unless we forgive, we will not be forgiven; for we have been forgiven a debt that we simply could not repay (the debt Christ paid for our sins); how unjust it would be for us, the beneficiaries of his mercy, to refuse to reciprocate and forgive those who have a lesser debt towards us. All we need to do is ask the Lord to bring to mind the image of anyone in our past or present whom He wants us to forgive, and to give us the grace to begin the walk towards letting go of all resentment towards that person, acceptance of the hurt he or she has caused us, and finally forgiveness. The reward of succeeding in this is freedom from the bitterness and darkness with which anger fills the soul.

Sloth is inordinate laziness. It is best described as profound indifference. English writer and poet Dorothy Sayers writes that sloth "believes in nothing, cares for nothing, seeks to know nothing, interferes with nothing, enjoys nothing, hates nothing, finds purpose in nothing, lives for nothing and remains alive because there is nothing for which it will die". Of course, there are degrees of sloth, and its offspring include procrastination, wasting time, useless activity, trivial conversation, the inability to contemplate (which is true leisure), weak-spiritedness, melancholy, and causeless irritation.

A good remedy for sloth is, first and foremost, to make sure to have a goal. The ultimate end of each person is eternal life in union with God, and our particular way of achieving that end is through our own unique vocation. We have to pray to be given the knowledge of that vocation and then live for it. If we have something to live for, we will avoid sloth.

A person disposed to sloth must force himself to do meaningful things, like volunteer work, helping those around us who cannot, for whatever reason, help themselves. We have to cultivate diligence and industriousness, which are habits that are really not difficult to cultivate. In fact, there is a danger that a person can become too functional or too caught up in his own "doing". What often happens is he begins to believe that God depends on his "doing", which is a delusion. The remedy in both cases is to learn to leisure properly. Genuine leisure is contemplation (of the highest things), and so the best remedy for sloth is to have regular times set aside for prayer and spiritual reading, that is, reading from the classics of the saints and doctors of the Church, such as St. Catherine of Siena, or St. Theresa of Avila, Father Jean Pierre de Caussade, etc.

Lust is inordinate sexual appetite. It is important to note that we are talking about disordered appetite. The sexual drive is not in itself evil, but good. Lust is the appetite for sexual pleasure that is contrary to the demands of human reason. Marriage is the proper context for the sexual act, since marriage is a joining of two, male and female, into one flesh. The sexual act is also a joining of two into one flesh, and so it is the act that consummates a marriage. Sexual union is the expression of married love, and it is an act that is in itself open to the procreation of new life. Outside of the context of marriage, the sexual act is neither unitive nor properly procreative (it can be reproductive, which is not the same as procreative), but is reduced to the pursuit of sexual gratification. It becomes a self-centered act, and using another sexually is very harmful both to one's own character and to the one being used.

The offspring of lust include spiritual blindness as well as a loss of interest in things spiritual; for one is so immersed in the flesh that the goods of the spirit lose their appeal. And because lust is so focused on pleasure, which exists in the self, the sexually disordered will lack a spirit of thoughtfulness. Obscenity is also an offspring of lust, and that includes obscene language as well as the production and interest in obscene literature. Immodest dress is an offspring of lust, for immodest dress manifests thoughtlessness, or worse, a desire to be the center of attention and an object of sexual desire. Moreover, because one is so focused on sexual pleasure, the lustful begin to despair of a future life. Lust is also accompanied by a hatred for the Church, which always stands for modesty and purity.

A remedy against lust is fasting. The reason is that gluttony, which includes dainty eating, will often generate a spirit of unchastity. There are degrees of fasting; one need not fast on bread and water for a full day, once or twice a week—although that might be a good idea for a while—, but regular sacrifices of certain foods, such as sweets, are important to keep the appetites from ruling over the intellect and will. If one is tempted sexually at the sight of a rather sexually appealing woman or man, one can change that temptation into something holy by turning the mind to God and praising Him for creating such a beautiful and desirable creature. Abstaining from alcohol is above all a very important precaution against lust, not to mention avoiding occasions and situations that render sexual self-control very difficult. Finally, spending a great deal of time in prayer before the Blessed Sacrament will certainly conquer the vice of lust.

The last of the capital sins is **gluttony**, which is inordinate appetite for food and drink. It is very difficult to draw the line allowing us to distinguish between the truly gluttonous and a healthy appetite. What is gluttony for a full grown adult will not necessarily be gluttonous for a teenager, and gluttony does not necessarily imply large quantities of food. Essentially, the glutton does not eat to live, he lives to eat. He is overly concerned with food. We really ought to be indifferent to food and eat for the sake of proper nourishment and health. Finding pleasure in food and drink is not sinful, but time should be used for the good of others, not for planning and executing delicious meals on a daily basis.

The offspring of gluttony include a loss of interest in things spiritual, as well as scurrility, which is unbecoming words; for one is so immersed in the physical that it becomes difficult to think before one speaks. Moreover, gluttony involves a disordered love of self, which leads to a loss of thoughtfulness and a delight in speaking that makes one the center of attention. Gluttony also leads to a dullness of the intellect. The remedy against gluttony is obviously fasting in one form or another. Simplicity in eating and the effort to cultivate indifference to food will overcome this particular vice and its offspring.

By the end of our lives, we should have learned that all that this world holds out to us with its promise that we will find perfect rest in these goods is really an illusion. As life progresses, we ought to become increasingly interior; for this life is about learning to love God and to find our neighbor within the very heart of God, and vice versa. Happiness is only found in dying to the self and awakening to the divine life that is in the very depths of the soul, for the most part hidden behind the darkness of a life blinded by disordered passion. We need to keep in mind that the goods and opportunities we sacrifice in this life, for the sake of His will, will all be returned to us if we achieve our destiny, which is union with God in the Beatific Vision, for God is the Supreme Good, and to possess God is to possess the fullness of unlimited goodness. Nothing is lacking in those who see God as He is in Himself. That is why it is so prudent to choose early on to engage in the battle against our own unique proclivities to sin and self-seeking. Outlined above are very specific ways to counter these proclivities, but the most general and powerful means of overcoming ourselves are regular Confession and Communion. Those who refuse to battle will be the greatest losers, for they are already defeated by their very choice to surrender to a life of sin, selfishness, and darkness.

A Note on the Value of Silence

You and I have a double interior. We can conceal what is within, that is, what is within our interior. A surgeon explores what is within you, yet you have concealed your deepest sentiments and intentions. He has not reached your interior. Why? The reason is that you have two interiors, and he has access to only one of them.

You have a spatial interior (your intestines are in you, your lunch is in you, etc), and you have a non-spatial interior, an immaterial interior, which is why the surgeon who explores your spatial interior will never uncover your deepest sentiments and intentions. He has no access to your "spiritual interior". A thought is within you, but it is not in your stomach, nor is it in your brain. No matter how thoroughly we explore your brain through X-Ray (brain scan), we will never discover your idea of the brain, or your idea of an idea, or your idea of your self, etc.,. A computer, however, has only a spatial interior; it does not possess a self-consciousness, because it has no self. It is a collection of individual substances unified into an artifact (it is an artificial product without a determinate nature or interior).

Sense perception opens us up onto the exterior world, which is replete with material substances that are sensible, that is, possessing affective qualities, such as color, sound, texture, odor, etc. Silence, however, allows us to descend into this supra-sensible interior, this immaterial realm within each one of us. But the senses cannot take us there; it is only through the power of intelligence through which one possesses self-consciousness that we make our way there. But why would anyone want to?

The reason is that this realm is a part of you. But more importantly, it is the deepest and most intimate part of you. You only share your deepest sentiments and intentions with the one you trust the most, for this realm is your most intimate sanctuary. If a person is uncomfortable in silence and when alone, then that person is uncomfortable with his or her deepest self. It is like being in a room with a stranger; often one will feel awkward, not sure what to say to the person, etc. If you are uncomfortable in silence and when alone with yourself, does that not imply that you are a stranger to yourself? That you only really know yourself through the behavior of others? That you depend for your identity upon how they might see and relate to you? And if so, is it any wonder that such peers can pressure you to do things that might in the end destroy you?

St. Theresa of Avila speaks of seven interiors, that is, seven mansions or rooms that make up the Interior Castle, which is the soul. The purpose of the spiritual life is to make it to that seventh mansion, because within that room, which is the Bridal chamber, one meets one's "eternal spouse". To discover merely the first room, the first mansion, is to discover that there is Someone (the totally Other) within one's deepest interior, and so one is moved to find Him, that is, one is moved to pray in silence and alone. Already, after entering this first mansion, one begins to discover oneself, and one discovers oneself to the degree that he or she descends more deeply into this interior, because soon we realize that our own self-discovery is inseparably connected to the discovery of this Someone who dwells within our deepest interior, who "created me for Himself", and "our hearts are restless until they rest in Thee, O Lord".

Silence is necessary because noise draws me out into the exterior world, which indeed is good and created by God, but this exterior world is not God. He dwells in the "heaven of the soul". I have to spend my life searching for this interior sun that burns within me, a sun that is covered by clouds, a mirror clouded by dirt and grime, but which when clean reflects my true image, that is, my true identity. To enter this seventh mansion is to find the deepest rest (peace) that one can possibly possess—and we are always seeking for rest. The problem with human beings is that they seek this rest in the finite goods of this world (beaches, hot spots, wealth, relationships, etc). These finite goods are genuine goods, but they do not and cannot quench a thirst that is infinite, and the human heart has an infinite thirst. Through lived experience one should discover—unless one lacks self-awareness, which many do indeed lack—that these finite goods do not satisfy, for the heart continues to thirst, to desire, to want. What is it looking for? It is looking for something that will impart rest. But only that which is proportioned to its thirst will give it rest, and if its thirst is infinite, then it is searching for the infinite, an object that it cannot circumscribe or contain, but an object that contains it, because it is larger than it, for it is larger than life, and it inspires and strikes an overwhelming sense of awe into it, because He is Beauty without limits, the source of all that is beautiful, good and true. Anything in this world that is true, good and beautiful pleases and fascinates the soul, but everything other than God possesses only a limited goodness, thus a limited splendor (beauty). Finite goods are only meant to draw one onward towards the source of all that is beautiful. But human beings, in the blindness caused by sin, impatience, lack of temperance, and inordinate love of self, seek their rest in the things of this world, and as a result they never find the peace that they are looking for. In fact, they only wound this world further by their sins, causing more hurt, more pain, more neurosis and stress related illnesses, and more confusion in the minds of the young. And when people become more restless, they become more desperate, and thus the search becomes more desperate, and the noise and clamor of the world increases.

But when you begin to see yourself through the eyes of Him who dwells within your deepest interior, through the eyes of Him who alone matters, you begin to see that although you really don't matter to the world, you do ultimately matter, because you matter to Him, and so it is His gaze that lifts you and fills you with a joy that the world cannot impart; for the world does not know you well, and the world will forget you, and above all, the world does not love you in any lasting and significant way. But He who alone matters has brought you into being for Himself, and the intimacy of marriage is only—and nothing more than—a step towards and preparation for an eternal "marriage" with God who resides deep within you, and who loves you as if there is only one of you.

Chapter 5: Some Fundamental Points on the Church, Petrine Authority, and Scripture

I've always said that one of the best things that can happen to a young Catholic is to room with a fiery non-Catholic Christian antithetical to Catholic doctrine. This can do a lot to force a Catholic out of his usual lukewarm complacency to defend his faith. Soon, however, he finds that he is unable to do so, because he does not know the faith, and this can move him to study it more fully in order to defend it.

One of the most basic points of contention about the Catholic faith concerns the authority of the Pope and bishops, what Catholics refer to as the Magisterium. Non-Catholics operate under the principle that Scripture alone is the sole rule of the faith, not any human being, or group of human beings, or tradition. How does a Catholic respond to this?

Firstly, if a person believes that Scripture is the word of God, then indirectly he or she acknowledges the authority of the Church. Why? Because Christ did not establish a bible, he established a Church, and the New Testament arose out of the very life of the Church.

Consider the gospel of Matthew, chapter sixteen. When Jesus went into the region of Caesarea Philippi he asked his disciples, "Who do people say that the Son of Man is?" They replied, "Some say John the Baptist, others Elijah, still others Jeremiah or one of the prophets." He said to them, "But who do you say that I am?" Simon Peter said in reply, "You are the Messiah (*Christos*), the Son of the living God." Jesus said to him in reply, "Blessed are you, Simon son of Jonah. For flesh and blood has not revealed this to you, but my heavenly Father. And so I say to you, you are Peter (*Petros*), and upon this rock (*petra*) I will build my church, and the gates of hell shall not prevail against it. I will give you the keys of the kingdom of heaven. Whatever you bind on earth shall be bound in heaven; and whatever you loose on earth shall be loosed in heaven." Then he ordered his disciples to tell no one that he was the Messiah.

We can learn a great deal about the papacy from this text. First of all, Jesus asked his disciples: "Who do people say that the Son of Man is?" Note the answers he received. None were correct. In other words, the truth about Christ does not come to us from the people. That is why the Church is not a democracy (from the Greek *demos*, which means "common people," and *kratos*, or rule).

Christ then asks them: "But who do you say that I am?" Simon speaks up and says "You are *Christos*, the Son of the living God." Jesus points out that it was not flesh and blood that revealed this to Peter. In other words, Peter did not figure this out through his own natural intelligence. It was revealed to him by the Father. In other words, the truth about God comes from God, not from man. Nevertheless, it comes to us *through* man; not just any man, but through that person the Father has chosen to preserve the truth about Himself revealed in the Person of Christ, in this case, Peter.

It is Peter who receives the keys of the kingdom. What are these "keys"? There is only one other place in Scripture where we see this image of the keys, and this is Isaiah, chapter twenty two:

Thus says the Lord, the God of hosts: Up, go to that official, Shebna, master of the palace, who has hewn for himself a sepulchre on a height and carved his tomb in the rock: "What are you doing here, and what people have you here, that here you have hewn for yourself a tomb?" The Lord shall hurl you down headlong, mortal man! He shall grip you firmly And roll you up and toss you like a ball into an open land to perish there, you and the chariots you glory in, you disgrace to your master's house! I will thrust you from your office and pull you down from your station.

On that day I will summon my servant Eliakim, son of Hilkiah; I will clothe him with your robe, and gird him with your sash, and give over to him your authority. He shall be a father to the inhabitants of Jerusalem, and to the house of Judah. I will place the key of the House of David on his shoulder; when he opens, no one shall shut, when he shuts, no one shall open. I will fix him like a peg in a sure spot, to be a place of honor for his family; On him shall hang all the glory of his family: descendants and offspring,...

The king of Israel had a cabinet of ministers, just as a Queen has her cabinet of ministers. From this cabinet, the king of Israel (the son of David) would appoint a first minister, or what we would today call a prime minister. This first minister was to be the master of the House of David, and so he would receive the key of the House of David. This key symbolizes authority as would the giving of keys to a person today also represent a kind of empowerment. The first minister was a father to the "inhabitants of Jerusalem". To be a "first minister" was to occupy an office, which means that the first minister can have a successor, as Eliakim succeeded Shebna.

Now Jesus is the true King of Israel who, in Matthew, selects his cabinet of ministers, twelve in number, to represent the New Israel—the first Israel was a nation of twelve tribes. From this cabinet Jesus selected a first minister, a "master of the palace", namely, Peter. He gave Peter the keys of the New House of David, the keys of the kingdom of God. Hence, Peter has a certain authority, and he is a father to the inhabitants of the New Jerusalem. The Italian word for father is *papa*, from which is derived the word "pope".

And finally, this station is an office, and so Peter will have successors, as Eliakim was the successor of Shebna. Furthermore, it is very possible for a person to hold this office unworthily—anyone who knows the history of the Church knows that there have been corrupt popes. But the office is clearly distinct from the person occupying it, as Shebna was corrupt and was to lose his position to Eliakim, who would assume the office.

Christ established a Church on the foundation stones of the twelve Apostles (see Eph 2, 20). The Apostles are the official teachers of the Church. They form that part of the Church that Catholics refer to as the Magisterium (from the Latin *magister*: chief, director).

The charism of infallibility is a gift given by Christ to the whole Church (see Jn, 16, 4-13). It is a gift that is ours, if we belong to his Mystical Body. Just as sight belongs to the entire living organism, yet requires an organ if the power of seeing is to be realized, so too the charism of infallibility that belongs to the entire Church requires an organ in order to be realized. This organ is the Magisterium, the official teachers of the Church, which is made up of the successors of the Apostles, that is, the bishops and Pope.

If we hold that Scripture is the word of God, we need only ask ourselves who it was that put together the canon of the New Testament in the first place. Or better yet, who wrote it? The gospels and epistles all came from the Church. They are the writings of the early Church, and it was the bishops of the Catholic Church that assembled the Canon—in the late 4th and early 5th centuries—and decided which books and letters were to be included and which ones would not be. To hold to the Scriptures as the word of God is to affirm the authority of the Church, at least indirectly; for the bible is really the Church's heirloom.

And so for the Catholic, there are three sources that constitute the rule of faith: the Magisterium, Sacred

Tradition, and Scripture. Christ established the Church, but the Church teaches in history, as the New Testament gives witness. In other words, Scripture is already the living tradition of the Church. As far as we know at this point, the first gospel written was Mark, written around 70 AD; a little later Matthew was written, followed by Luke. The gospel of John was written near the end of the first century, and it reads very differently than the first three synoptic gospels, and Matthew is very different from Luke. What they give witness to is the living historical tradition of the Church. It is the living Church in history who teaches, and she teaches the truth. We know this because Christ promised this to the Church. If we turn to John, chapter fourteen, we read: "I will ask the Father and he will give you another Paraclete—to be with you always: the Spirit of truth, whom the world cannot accept, since it neither sees him nor recognizes him; ..." (14, 16). Also, a little further on we read: "When he comes, however, being the Spirit of truth he will guide you to all truth" (16, 13).

What we need to remember here is that John is reacting to the heresy of Gnosticism, which denied the goodness of the flesh; Gnostics denied that God created matter, and so they denied that God would become incarnate in Jesus. That is why John emphasizes the goodness of the body throughout the gospel; i.e., note the story of the doubting Thomas, how Christ invites him to touch his hands and his side. All throughout the gospel of John we are reminded of the goodness of matter.

The point here is that Christ could not have been referring to individuals when he said "the Spirit of Truth will lead you to all truth". The Gnostics did not have the truth. Christ was referring to the Church that he established. He commissioned the twelve to go out to all nations and teach all that he taught them: "Full authority has been given to me both in heaven and on earth; go, therefore, and make disciples of all the nations. Baptize them in the name 'of the Father and of the Son and of the Holy Spirit.' Teach them to carry out everything I have commanded you. And know that I am with you always, until the end of the world!" (Mt 28, 18-20).

It is this command to go out to the whole world (all nations) that marks the Church that Christ established, which is why that Church came to be known as "Catholic", from the Greek word *katholikos* (*kata* "about", and *holos*, "whole"). Early in the second century, not even fifteen years after the book of Revelation was written, while on his way to execution, St. Ignatius of Antioch wrote: "Where the bishop is present, there let the congregation gather, just as where Jesus Christ is, there is the Catholic Church".[10] The Church believes that when the bishops speak as teachers, Christ speaks; for he said to them: "He who hears you, hears me; and he who rejects you, rejects me" (Lk 10, 16).

St. Paul in his letters also warns the faithful to hold fast to the tradition they received: "We command you, brothers, in the name of the Lord Jesus Christ, to avoid any brother who wanders from the straight path and does not follow the tradition you received from us" (2 Th 3, 6).

The Church is a body, and a living body is characterized by unity. It is organized, as all organisms are. But a corpse decomposes. We are members of a larger body, and it is not for us to separate ourselves from this living body because we see things differently from the official teachers of the Church. St. Paul urges the faithful: "Make every effort to preserve the unity which has the Spirit as its origin and peace as its binding force. There is one Lord, one faith, one baptism; one God and Father of all…" (Eph 4, 3-5).

The Christian faith is an ecclesial faith. St. Paul points out that prophecy, although a charism belonging to an individual through which the Holy Spirit manifests himself, is subject to the judgment of the larger community: "Let no more than two or three prophets speak, and let the rest judge the worth of what they say" (1 Co 14, 29).

There is an obvious problem with dissent that is based on the principle of *sola scriptura*. The non-Catholic Christian reads the bible and insists that the bible is the sole rule of his faith. As is often the case, he comes up with an entirely different interpretation from that of the official Church. But some other lady reads the same bible and comes up with an interpretation entirely opposed to the other two. So far we have three people, and three different interpretations. Given four hundred people reading the same bible and interpreting it on their own authority, we end up with four hundred different and often conflicting versions of Christianity. One person believes Jesus is God the Son, fully God and fully man, but another denies it, insisting that he is not equal to the Father and that he's merely, but God is present in him in a special way. Another says Jesus is God; he has a divine nature, but not a real human nature. One insists that it is good to pray for the dead, another denies it. One says it is good to pray to saints, others say no. Who is right? They can't all be right. Who is going to settle the dispute? Certainly not the bible. Who has the correct interpretation of the bible?

The bible arose out of the very life and heart of the Church; it belongs to her as a whole. That is why in the early Church, when disputes arose—and they certainly did arise—, it was the bishops of the Church who gathered together from all around the empire to form an ecumenical council (i.e., the Council of Nicea, the Council of Chalcedon, Council of Ephesus, etc.), and Rome would have the final say. What the bishops of the

Church taught was "official". Without that authority, there's nothing left but confusion and a myriad of conflicting opinions. As St. Paul says: "...God is a God, not of confusion, but of peace" (1 Co 14, 33). The Holy Spirit can't be inspiring all of them; for truth does not conflict with itself. So which one has the truth? Consider what St. Irenaeus, an early Christian Father, wrote in the middle of the 2nd Century:

Having received this preaching and this faith, as I had said, the Church, although scattered in the whole world, carefully preserves it, as if living in one house. She believes these things everywhere alike, as if she had but one heart and one soul, and preaches them harmoniously, teaches them, and hands them down, as if she had but one mouth. For the languages of the world are different, but the meaning of the Christian tradition is one and the same. Neither do the churches that have been established in Germany believe otherwise, or hand down any other tradition, nor those among the Iberians, nor those among the Celts, nor in Egypt, nor in Libya, nor those established in the middle parts of the world. But as God's creature, the sun is one and the same in the whole world, so also the preaching of the truth shines everywhere, and illumines all men who wish to come to the knowledge of the truth. Neither will one of those who preside in the churches who is very powerful in speech say anything different from these things, for no one is above his teacher, nor will one who is weak in speech diminish the tradition. For since the faith is one and the same, he who can say much about it does not add to it, nor does he who can say little diminish it....[11]

Much later on, in the same work, St. Irenaeus writes:

Since, however, it would be very tedious, in such a volume as this, to reckon up the successions of all the

Churches, we do put to confusion all those who, in whatever manner, whether by an evil self-pleasing, by vainglory, or by blindness and perverse opinion, assemble in unauthorized meetings; we do this, I say, by indicating that tradition derived from the apostles, of the very great, the very ancient, and universally known Church founded and organized at Rome by the two most glorious apostles, Peter and Paul; as also by pointing out the faith preached to men, which comes down to our time by means of the successions of the bishops. For it is a matter of necessity that every Church should agree with this Church, on account of its pre-eminent authority, that is, the faithful everywhere, inasmuch as the apostolic tradition has been preserved continuously by those faithful men who exist everywhere.[12]

It should be pointed out that there is also such a thing as "internal dissent" that is a bit more difficult to detect. We have witnessed this kind of dissent since the Second Vatican Council (1962). Some people within the Catholic Church have taken a different path. Now, in itself, there is nothing wrong with this, for there have been many reform movements throughout the history of the Church, which began with certain people taking a new path or walking down a new road (i.e., Francis of Assisi, monastic reforms, etc.). Not all reform movements, however, remained faithful to Peter. Today there are people who many years earlier took a turn onto a trail that was thought to be the one the Church as a whole was treading. They felt that because they were able to detect movement in the Church, they were able to discern its direction. Many of these people regarded themselves as "prophets", in a manner of speaking, and although they did not visibly leave the Church, what they taught contained genuine elements of Catholic teaching yet stripped of so much that characterizes mainstream

Catholicism. Their agenda also seemed to include attitudes and elements antithetical to the teaching authority of the Church.

What happened was that eventually the Church began to articulate and clearly delineate a post-Vatican II understanding of herself. We saw this in the Encyclicals and writings of Pope John Paul II, as well as the 1994 *Catechism of the Catholic Church*, which the Holy Father (John Paul II) said is "a sure norm for teaching the faith and thus a valid and legitimate instrument for ecclesial communion." What we eventually came to see was that some trails really did express the direction in which the Church as a whole was moving, while others turned out to be "a wrong turn". It is no coincidence that those new paths that proved true to the Church had always stressed the importance of fidelity and loyalty not just to Scripture, but to Tradition and Magisterium. Those that proved defective regarded much of Church Tradition as outdated and irrelevant—and mistakenly thought Vatican II did so as well—and regarded the authority of ecclesiastical office, especially that of the Pope, as merely human and derived ultimately from academic achievement.

The problem, however, is that when a person or group of persons takes a wrong turn and the longer one proceeds down that road, the more difficult it becomes to acknowledge that one has made a wrong turn, back up, return to the original spot and proceed on the right road, unfortunately behind many others who stayed the course. This is especially difficult for those who regarded themselves as prophets of a new age in the Church. What happens is such people will shout all the louder, all the while moving farther from the point at which they veered off course, their voices becoming less and less audible, until they are no longer heard from.

This has given rise to an interesting phenomenon. Because many non-Catholic Christians are seriously devoted to Scripture as the inspired word of God, such as those old fashioned Baptists or Evangelicals, many of them seem more identifiably Catholic than the internal dissenters who remain within the walls of the Catholic Church. In other words, these "bible Christians" often have far more in common with mainstream Catholicism and more to share with mainstream Catholics than those who hopped on the bandwagon of internal dissent that was on the move just after Vatican II.

Miracles and the Dangers of Rationalism

I was once asked the following questions via email from someone I'd never met: "Does a Catholic need to believe in the miracles of Christ according to the Gospels? Is it against the Church's teaching to teach grade school children that the miracles of Christ are not historically true?"

There is no doubt that it is contrary to the faith of the Church to maintain that the miracles of Christ are not historically true; for the Church has always held that the miracles of Christ are historically true. To teach kids the contrary is nothing short of "scandalizing the little ones" who believe in him, something that Christ gave us a severe warning about (Mt 18, 6). Revelation always involves both words and deeds. Let me quote from Vatican II: "the deeds wrought by God in the history of salvation manifest and confirm the teaching and realities signified by the words, while the words proclaim the deeds and clarify the mystery contained in them" (DV 2). As Theologian Germain Grisez writes: "Not all the words and deeds can constitute divine revelation, but only those that can be recognized as a personal communication from God and that the recipient, if reasonable, will accept as such. So, at least some of the deeds must be mighty and wondrous--miraculous events that, because immanent causes cannot account for them,

87

can be recognized as divine signs, signals from the creator, God's signature on the message."[13]

There is a school of thought that was popular in the 60s that is heavily influenced by German philosopher Georg Wilhelm Friedrich Hegel (the most polite atheist in the history of philosophy). Hegel was a rationalist. He argued that philosophy (human reason) can fully understand and explicate the tenets of religious faith. In fact, only when philosophy has done so are the tenets of religion fully understood, he thought. In other words, faith, in his mind, does not transcend reason. The problem, however, is that there are many things in the Scriptures that simply cannot be reconciled with Hegel's philosophy, such as the transcendence of God, God's free decision to bring things other than Himself into existence, the perfection and unchanging nature of God, the Trinity, the Incarnation of the Second Person of the Trinity (at least as it was understood in the first and second centuries of the Church), the miracles of Christ, in particular the resurrection, etc. In consequence, Hegel and his followers subject these to deconstruction, or demythologization.

Hans Kueng (Kung), who is probably Hegel's most popular disciple, labors to portray himself as one who has adopted the middle position between the two extremes of what he calls "fundamentalism" on the one hand, and rationalism on the other. Much of what he writes concerning the purpose of the miracle narratives in Scripture is true, but in the end, his deconstructionism unveils nothing less than a thoroughgoing rationalism, which Kueng somehow believes he has avoided. As an example, he writes: "The story of the calming the storm, for instance, may have originated in a rescue from distress at sea after prayer and a call for help. The story of the coin in the fish's mouth may be based on Jesus' request to catch a fish in order to pay the temple tax." His rationalism is particularly evident in his treatment of the resurrection. He writes: "Corporeal resurrection? Yes and no, …No, if "body" simply means the physiological identical body. Yes, if "body" means in the sense of the New Testament soma the identical personal reality, the same self with its whole history."

The irony in Kueng's position, however, is that the biblical term *soma* means precisely the entire person in his corporeal identity. For a Jew, if there is no physical or bodily resurrection literally speaking, there is simply no resurrection; for **you are your body**. Faith in the bodily resurrection does not amount to fundamentalism any more than does faith in the Incarnation. Rather, it is the only conceivable position that follows from the non-dualist anthropology that regards matter as belonging to the very essence of man. A bodiless human person is nothing more than a dead one. Kueng's position is not the mean between extremes, but the extreme of unbelief disguised as a balanced compromise. The notion of the resurrection simply does not fit into the Hegelian framework of the necessary and dialectical evolution of the Absolute, ultimately identified with the whole of the physical universe (Hegel's pantheism).

It is possible for God, who is distinct from and the author of creation, to bring about an event that is outside the order of the laws of nature, that is, work a miracle, if He so chooses. This is especially true if Jesus is the Incarnation of the Son, the Second Person of the Trinity. If all things came to be through the Word (Jn 1, 1): "And God said, "Let there be…and there was…"" (Gn 1, 1-31), and if Jesus is the Word who came into the world (Jn 1, 10), then the move from faith in the Incarnation to faith in the fact that Jesus spoke and the "wind and the sea obey him" (Mk 4, 41) is not a difficult step to take. Miracles are only difficult for the person who has chosen not to believe in them. Indeed the Greek word for "miracle" means "sign", and thus miracles are signs of the kingdom. But there is no signifying without a real existing sign. If Jesus did not actually heal the physical blindness of the blind man at Bethsaida, or actually heal the man with a withered hand, or cure Peter's mother-in-law, then nothing is actually signified. One cannot receive a ticket for driving above the speed limit that is signified by a sign that does not actually exist.

Teaching anyone, let alone young children, that the miracle accounts in Scripture did not happen can do nothing but destroy faith. The damage resulting from such an approach is incalculable. People need the permission to believe above all, and they get that permission from seeing mature adults with real faith. Some people, however, are so hung up on appearing and feeling sophisticated that they simply cannot find the humility to stand before others with the heart of a child that believes.

Concluding Thoughts

It is best to remember that the Church operates according to an ancient working principle: *lex orandi, lex credendi*, which means "the law of praying" is the "law of believing". In other words, how the Church prays is a reflection of what the Church believes. That is why in order to understand what the Church truly believes, historians will look to the ancient liturgy, that is, how the Church prayed.

But how does the Church come to know? She knows what to believe because She knows herself, that is, She knows how She is inclined to worship. The Church is not just a bunch of men who went to school, got degrees, and are now considered the experts. Individual persons are not infallible, even the best of theologians and Doctors of the Church—the only individual who is infallible is the successor of Peter, when he speaks *ex cathedra* on matters of faith and morals. He is *primus supra pares*, not *primus inter pares* (He is the first above equals, not the first among equals). This, however, is a charism of office, not something that belongs to him by virtue of his education or personal accomplishments.

But it is the Church as a whole that knows Herself and Her own inclination, which is expressed in Her liturgy; for the Church as a whole is Christ's Mystical Body, and She prays. The Church lives in Christ and is One Body in Christ, her Bridegroom. The Holy Spirit is the very soul of the Church, and the Church prays in history, throughout the centuries. In her, heaven and earth join, because in the Person of Christ heaven and earth were joined hypostatically, the human and divine natures joined in the One Person (hypostasis) of the Son. Heaven and earth continue to be joined in Her faith, the faith of the Church, and in Her prayer, that is, in the liturgy. She is a believing and praying Church, and Her self-understanding is rooted there. Theologians are simply called to serve that faith; they have no dominion over it. They must be part of that faith in order to come to genuine theological understanding, that is, they must be a part of the believing Church vivified by the Holy Spirit in order to be theologians. All their judgments are subject to the teaching office, the Magisterium, which is the organ of that charism of infallibility that Christ promised to the Church and which belongs to Her as a whole. In fact, many of the great doctors of the Church would explicitly preamble their writings with such a condition, leaving everything they wrote ultimately up to the judgment of the Church.

The reason that it is so important to have a Magisterium is precisely in the relationship between liturgy and faith (*lex orandi, lex credendi*). Error in faith will inevitably impact on how a person worships, that is, how one prays, and how one prays inevitably impacts on how one lives and loves. Everything in the Church serves love, and genuine prayer carries us into the depths of God's presence where we find the world that God so deeply loves. Worship and intercession are bound together in a single reality. That is why orthodoxy is ultimately a matter of such grave importance.

Finally, it is one thing to look at the nature of the Church theologically and from a relatively general and abstract point of view, but when we are part of that institution, we inevitably come up against the **humanness** of the Church. The Church is made up of human beings who have to pray daily: "...forgive us our trespasses as we forgive those who trespass against us." This fact is nothing other than an extension of God's humility; He chooses to communicate Himself through the instrumentality of matter (sacraments), and human persons are material things. Christ perpetuates his sacrifice throughout history through the unworthy hands of sinful human persons, and he also preserves the deposit of faith through the sinful and frail instruments of human bishops.

When we live the spiritual life within the Church, we come up against all sorts of neuroses, emotional sickness, pride, insecurities, jealousies, envy, fear, narcissism, cowardliness, etc. The priesthood, unfortunately, has attracted all sorts of undesirable characters—and the institution has not always been that careful in screening them out—because the priest, after all, is from one angle a center of attention every week, in the context of a liturgy (he should not be, of course, but all eyes are on him). For some priests, the parish is his own little fiefdom and everyone else his serfs—he cannot free others because he himself is not free; some turn the liturgy into a little show, dotted with light bantering that call attention to his "cute" idiosyncrasies, creating as many opportunities for applause as is possible within the span of a one hour liturgy; some delight in the liturgy as a narcissist delights in the stage.

Or, we find priests who are as sanctimonious as the characters they read about in their legend filled lives of saints. Indeed, such people have ceased to be men—or never grew out of adolescence to become men in the first place. They have lost a moral thickness and depth, and they are no longer grounded and living in the realm of the real, but in the safe and comforting dreamland of their own imaginations.

In both scenarios, there is a lack of missionary zeal, because a true missionary does not pursue his own ends, devoting all his energies to maintaining the comfortable delusions he has about himself. He is focused primarily and exclusively on the salvation of souls; he can free others because he himself has been set free by Christ. He has not "set himself apart", rendering himself relatively inaccessible, as a result of a "Phariseeism" that never seems to die, one dressed in new garb and cleverly fabricated through an abuse of a theology founded on the principle of *in persona Christi*. Rather, those with a genuine missionary spirit are "set apart" (sacred) as a result of their extraordinary charity, courage, and humility, that is, their deep rooted conviction that they are no better than anyone and their willingness to enter into the sufferings of others in order to bring light and life to their darkness.

In the real world of the Church, we run into neurotic characters more often than we do the genuine missionaries. But we have to learn to get past that, to acquire eyes for the Lord, eyes that are trained to see Christ under his many unsightly and unpleasant disguises. It has been said that the Church must be guided by the Holy Spirit, for if she were not, the clergy would have destroyed the Church centuries ago. Theological ideas, however beautiful they might be, do not succeed in purifying human beings; only human beings purify other human beings, and we purify one another by learning to put up with one another, learning to be patient with one another, to pray for one another, to seek forgiveness from one another. Purification is difficult, but the more we are purified, the easier it becomes to spot the Lord hiding behind the humanness of his unworthy instruments; for we can spot him there because we have discovered him in ourselves, and we know ourselves as highly unworthy instruments.

Chapter 6: Liberal and Conservative: Two Terms That Have No Place in Catholic Theology

Recently a student of mine sent me a series of questions she plans to ask me during an interview she's conducting as part of an English assignment. In one of her questions, she asks whether my theological views are "liberal, midstream, or conservative".

I was surprised at the question, because my students typically do not think in those terms; most, in fact, are barely familiar with them even in their current political setting. 14 Nevertheless, "liberal" and "conservative" are political terms that we do not find in the history of Catholic theology, or in the writings of the Fathers or the great Doctors of the Church. They were brought into the realm of Catholicism, relatively recently, by some as a way of legitimizing their dissent from Church teaching, especially in the area of morality.

Being a liberal or a conservative in the political realm is legitimate in a democracy, because politics is a branch of ethics, and ethics is principally about prudence. The virtue of prudence is about the application of universal principles to particular situations. Hence, prudence requires an understanding of universal principles as well as a host of virtues that can only arise out of a rich experience of concrete situations that contain so many variables, virtues such as circumspection, foresight, shrewdness, memory, docility, and caution.

Political prudence is a virtue that is developed over a long period of time, after a great deal of experience, a knowledge of history, an understanding of the nature of the human person, as well as a thorough understanding of the laws of economics. And because prudential judgments bear upon concrete particulars, they are not always so clear and certain. That is why docility is an integral part of prudence. A person might have greater

95

foresight as a result of his experience, or a better memory, or greater circumspection, and thus might notice important details that we might have overlooked. And so we can expect people to be more or less right and left leaning, in the realm of politics. Some argue that more government intervention is, at certain times, necessary, while others put forth the argument that less government intervention will accomplish more for the poor and the civil community as a whole in the long run. Politics is not and never has been a black and white affair.

But try looking for "liberal", "conservative", "left" and "right" in the great variety of theology that we find in the writings of the Fathers and Doctors of the Church, for example. What we find there are a variety of theologies seeking to understand the same deposit from different and even newer angles, but all of them consistent with the faith of the Church. Had anything been found in their writings that was contrary to the faith of the Church, it was not placed on a spectrum in the space of a window of dissent; it was simply condemned. "Left" and "right" do not exist as meaningful theological terms in the history of Catholic theology.

The 1960s witnessed all sorts of dissent—from the Church's moral teaching in particular—, and in order to legitimize this dissent in their minds, those unfaithful to the teachings of the Church adopted the labels "liberal" and "conservative", "left" and "right", which gave the appearance that their particular leanings were less unorthodox— not to mention heretical—as they were justifiably "left", like their political counterparts.

And so the 40 year period after Vatican II was increasingly characterized by a kind of cult of ambiguity and moral indeterminacy. The less certain a person sounded, the more mature and sophisticated was he considered to be, and the more clear, certain and determinate a person was on moral issues, the less credibility he enjoyed.

The creation of the *Catechism of the Catholic Church* as well as the clear and definite pronouncements of two great popes is gradually rendering such political terms as applied to a Catholic theology, as well as the mentality that seeks to hide its infidelity and unorthodoxy behind them, a thing of the past.

Chapter 7: A Clarification on the Meaning of "Conscience"

Whenever I think certain popular misconceptions are finally behind us, someone who should know better, such as a priest, teacher, or God forbid, a bishop, brings me back to reality. One such misconception that seems to never go away is the idea that conscience is the final arbiter of what is morally right—a misconception often designated under the expression "primacy of conscience".

But to put it bluntly, conscience is not the final arbiter of what is morally right, nor has the Church ever taught that it is. In its truest sense, conscience is the intellectual apprehension of the Divine Law. For this reason, Divine Law is primary.

In his Letter to the Duke of Norfolk, Newman quotes Cardinal Gousset, who writes: "The Divine Law is the supreme rule of actions; our thoughts, desires, words, acts, all that man is, is subject to the domain of the law of God; and this law is the rule of our conduct by means of our conscience. Hence it is never lawful to go against our conscience."

Essentially, conscience is one's best judgment, in a given situation, on what here and now is to be done as good, or to be avoided as evil. Because conscience is one's best judgment, *hic et nunc*, a person has a duty to obey it. The Fourth Lateran Council says: "He who acts against his conscience loses his soul".

Moreover, the duty to obey one's conscience includes an erroneous conscience. For example, if, as a result of being brought up by neurotic parents, I judge that in this particular situation right now, drinking this cup of coffee is contrary to God's will, then I have a duty not to drink the cup of coffee. Should the Pope or a local Bishop try to persuade me that there is nothing sinful in drinking a cup of coffee and yet for some reason I continue to judge, erroneously, that drinking this cup of coffee would offend my Creator, I must nonetheless follow my conscience and not drink the coffee. The reason is that if I were to drink it, I'd be doing what in my best judgment is morally wrong.

This is what is meant by the "primacy of conscience", that is, conscience having the final word on what I ought to do in the here and now situation.

"Primacy of conscience" does not mean that I can dissent from Church teaching on a particular issue because I don't agree with the teaching or see anything wrong with doing what the Church says I ought not to do. That this is true is rather easy to demonstrate.

Let us say that I regularly engage in a particular behavior that I think is perfectly innocent, such as telling certain off-color jokes to a classroom of teenagers, and my conscience does not bother me in the slightest when doing so. Clearly, my conscience is deficiently formed. But one day a colleague approaches and says: "I think what you are doing is unprofessional, but I can't explain it now, I've got to run for an appointment. We'll talk later." At this point I am rather surprised, and I begin to consider my friend's character and past judgments. I know he's not trying to manage my life and that he generally gives a great deal of thought to what he holds to be morally right or wrong.

Already my conscience has been altered, even though my friend had no time to explain himself to me. When I find myself in a situation in which I am about to tell these jokes, my judgment bearing upon the act is now different as a result of my colleague's remarks. Here and now I know that choosing to tell these off-color jokes might very well be morally wrong—although at this point I don't quite understand how—, because my friend whom I know to be reasonable told me that it is wrong. My best judgment at this point is that "perhaps I should wait and think about this further".

For me to proceed with the jokes because I enjoy making people laugh and judge that doing so is morally okay is not good enough at this point; for I know that I have been wrong in the past, and so I know my judgment might now be mistaken.

If this is true for a colleague, how much more so for the Vicar of Christ himself, or the formulated teachings of the Church that was established not by man, but by the God-man, who sent the Holy Spirit to lead his Church to the complete truth (Jn 16, 13) and who said to the apostles: "He who hears you, hears me" (Lk 10, 16), and who said to Peter: "Whatever you bind on earth shall be considered bound in heaven; whatever you loose on earth shall be considered loosed in heaven" (Mt 16, 19)?

The only time I can reasonably act against my friend's counsel is if I judge, here and now, that were I not to tell those jokes to students, I would be doing what in my best judgment is sinful. If, for example, a Catholic claims to be able to choose *In Vitro Fertilization* in good conscience while knowing that the Church teaches that such an option is morally wrong, it must mean that he or she is convinced that it would be sinful not to choose that option. That would certainly constitute an erroneous conscience; nevertheless, he or she would be obliged to obey it.

For the most part, however, this is not what people claim when they act contrary to Church teaching. Rather, many simply choose to dissent, and they hide their dissent behind the catchphrase "primacy of conscience". But conscience does not mean that Catholics are free to act on the basis of what they personally judge is morally right in spite of Church teaching. Catholic conversion, as the etymology of "conversion" indicates, means a complete turnaround (*vertere*), implying movement in a new direction in conjunction with (con) the community of Christ's

Mystical Body. As St. Paul says: "We all were among them too in the past, living sensual lives, ruled entirely by our own physical desires and our own ideas" (Eph 2, 3). But, we have become a new creation (Gal 6, 13). Bishops and priests who have been exposed to the rich theological heritage that is ours in the Church have no excuse for employing a version of "conscience" which, in the final analysis, undercuts their very authority.

Chapter 8: Reclaiming Catholic Social Teaching

Catholic social teaching is a magnificent body of doctrine that stems from the Church's understanding of herself as Christ's Bride redeemed, as his Mystical Body vivified by the Holy Spirit. Her rich social doctrine exhibits continuity with every other aspect of her formulated teaching, for the Popes speak from the reservoir of the entire Catholic tradition, that is, from the very heart of the believing Church. This is not always evident, however, when her social doctrine is presented through the filters of the typical "social justice" activist.

The reason for this, it seems to me, is that many "social justice" advocates approach Catholic social teaching from an entirely different angle than the popes of the major social encyclicals of the twentieth century. A large percentage of these activists were at one time in their lives devotees of Karl Marx, and although some of them have left strict Marxism behind, they continue to approach both social problems and Catholic social teaching within a Marxist *habitus*, an intellectual disposition that determines what it is they see as important and worthy of emphasis in Catholic social teaching. The result is often a very dilapidated doctrine that is left leaning, misleading, and lacks the fullness exhibited in the encyclicals. Allow me to attempt a brief summary of the essential points of Marxism in order to clarify what I mean.

Brief Summary of Marxism

Marxism is often referred to as a dialectical materialism. This means that reality is nothing but matter, which in turn is in a perpetual state of becoming. Dialectic describes a process in which opposites enter into conflict with one another. The result of this tension is that one side negates the other, giving rise to a new synthesis. For Marx, history is essentially a dialectical process.

Historical conflict bears upon man's activity, the basic form of which is manual labour. Man, according to Marx, develops himself through labour, but certain economic structures and labour relations impede his development and alienate him from his product, which is a reflection of himself. This alienating system, according to Marx, is Capitalism, for within this wage labour system, the product of a man's labour does not belong to him.

In response, the working class seeks to recover itself, to overcome this alienation, and according to Marx it can do so only through a social revolution through which it abolishes private property and brings about the transition to communism (a new synthesis).

It is important to keep in mind that in Marxism, the basic historical reality is not the individual person, who for us exists in the image and likeness of God, and who is endowed with a spiritual and immortal soul. Rather, the basic historical reality is, for Marx, **social man** in his economic activity in nature. The individual is merely a part of social man. He wrote: "In its reality it [the essence of man] is the ensemble of social relations." And so Marxism concerns itself primarily with social acts, not acts that lack an immediate and obvious social significance.

Furthermore, it is the labour of social man, his specific method of production and the economic relations it generates that determine the form of political life, the content of law, and the prevailing morality of the period, not vice versa. It is not that the individual person is able to apprehend the nature of things, such as human nature, or the nature of the state, or the nature of moral conduct and law, thus allowing him to establish a legal infrastructure that is true to natural law and that establishes, in part, the conditions in which individual persons can flourish. Rather, ideas, including religious ideas, are determined by the specific economic relations and conditions that prevail in a society. Moreover, history is in process, and so too, therefore, are human ideas. Thus, for Marx, there are no "eternal verities" or absolute truths.

In a capitalist society, according to Marx, law, social structures, morality, current ideas, etc, are all shaped by the dominant class (exploiters/oppressors) for the sake of maintaining power. But such morality has no more objectivity than a fable. Communist morality, on the other hand, is characterized by the revolutionary imperative. In 1920, Lenin wrote: "...for the communist, morality lies entirely in this compact, united discipline and conscious mass struggle against the exploiters. We do not believe in an eternal morality, ...we say: morality is what serves to destroy the old exploiting society and to unite all the toilers around the proletariat, which is creating a new communist society...Morality serves the purpose of helping human society to rise to a higher level and to get rid of the exploitation of labour."[15]

Marxist ethics is an ethics of results. There is no such thing as an act being intrinsically evil or having intrinsic goodness. The goodness and evil of acts are measured by the degree to which they further the cause of the self-emancipation of the oppressed class. So, intentionally killing another human being is not "intrinsically" evil, for one may hang capitalists "from the nearest lampposts", said Marx; doing so only furthers the historical movement towards final emancipation.

Combine this with the fact that for Marx, the basic historical reality is social man, it is obvious why the fundamental virtues of a Marxist worldview are class solidarity, hatred of all oppression, discipline, and devotion to the construction of a classless and communist world.[16]

Latent Marxism

The more familiar we become with the ideas of Marx, the easier it is to detect its presence under the guise of a Catholic social justice ethics. The first indication of the Marxist *habitus* lurking behind a particular rendering of Catholic social teaching is the habit of thinking in polemical terms: exploited/exploiter, oppressed/oppressor, etc. and the resulting habit of thinking within an anti-establishment mentality. Thus, the institutional Church, in so far as it is a wealthy establishment, is regarded in a negative light. Relations of male/female, clergy/laity are almost always interpreted polemically as well.

Another indication of a Marxist undercurrent is the conspicuous absence of personal morality, and thus an exclusive emphasis on the social. It is as if the personal and the social are discontinuous, as they were for Marx. For many who see themselves as social justice advocates, issues like fornication, abortion, contraception, and other life issues, are not worthy of serious consideration, for these are regarded as private acts, not social acts of a certain class (the oppressor or exploiter).

The Magisterium, on the other hand, always underscores the link between "social" injustices and the personal: "The root and font of this defection in economic and social life from the Christian law, and of the consequent apostasy of great numbers of workers from the Catholic faith, are the disordered passions of the soul, the sad result of original sin which has so destroyed the wonderful harmony of man's faculties that, easily led astray by his evil desires, he is strongly incited to prefer the passing goods of this world to the lasting goods of Heaven".[17]

105

Another clue is the adoption of Consequentialism (the moral goodness of human acts are determined by consequences, thus one may do evil that good may come of it); for the rejection of a natural law morality is part of the adoption of a Marxist "ethics of results". One can sometimes detect an ironic blend of moral relativism and absolutism in typical social justice parlance, an inconsistency very present in Marxism. For example, consider the absolute and automatic condemnation of all Western military action, but relative silence in the face of the military action of terrorists or Leftists.

One also finds the tendency to regard the poor universally as victims of unjust social conditions—which is, of course, why any violence or military action on their part is not so repugnant. Marx believed in the natural goodness of the individual and held that everything that was wrong in the world was the result of environmental conditions. Evil, in other words, originates not in the heart, but in the "system". Accordingly, criminals too are merely victims of unjust social conditions.

The parallel is that since, in the context of the Church, evil does not exist on the level of the person, it isn't so much the person who needs healing as much as hierarchical structures need abolishing, which is why there is often very little emphasis, if any, on the sacraments, individual Confession, the Eucharist, devotions, etc., and a favoring of almost anything that will contribute in some way to abolishing the distinction between the royal priesthood of the faithful and the ministerial priesthood.

Another indication of latent Marxism is the presence of historical progressivism. What is latest is always regarded as better in so far as history is moving towards "the kingdom of man deified" (the post communist golden age). Hence, those Catholic activists who find it regressive to maintain a connection with the past, and why many social justice textbooks, newspapers, or programs lack any visible connection with traditional Catholicism. There is also the tendency, originally present in Marx, to label the opposition as "reactionary", among other more derogatory labels. The rise of Mariology, moreover, is often explained away as a purely natural and historical phenomenon that has its roots in an historical polemic of one kind or another, reminiscent of the Marxist view that ideas arise from and are understood in light of economic structures and the relations they generate.

In typical social justice parlance, we rarely, if ever, come across the expression "works of mercy", either corporal or spiritual. It seems that acts formerly understood as corporal works of mercy (i.e., to feed the hungry; to give drink to the thirsty; to clothe the naked; to visit the sick; etc.) have now been subsumed under the designation "justice". It is as if anyone who has been blessed with wealth is no longer part of the oppressed class, and so is automatically part of the class of oppressors. And so what he does with his excess wealth is no longer a matter of mercy or charity, but justice. But one does not encounter this mentality in the encyclicals.

The Marxist or semi Marxist approach to social justice can be attractive and is even described by some as "liberating". This liberation, however, might be nothing more than the feeling of not having to grapple with personal sin and reform in so far as the focus now is almost exclusively on social sin.

But one clue that a rendering of Catholic social teaching proceeds from the heart of the Church is that Christ is proclaimed, not so much as a first century peace activist, but as Saviour and Lord who alone heals human brokenness and who alone ushers in the kingdom of God, which is not of this world. All our good works are nothing more than a gathering of wood and other materials that we lay at the feet of Christ in the hope that he will take these and transform them into a beautiful edifice: "Unless the Lord build the house, in vain do the builders labour" (Ps 127, 1).

Some Final Points on Subsidiarity and the Limits of Human Intelligence

It seems that many people today—including Catholics faithful to Catholic teaching and those not entirely so—have a tendency to pronounce on matters of economic policy with little more than very general moral principles of love and generosity, and a general knowledge of man's personal and relational nature, etc. The problem, however, is that there is too great a gap between the two levels of abstraction (that of a theological anthropology and the science of economics, which is the study of the allocation of scarce resources that have alternative uses). Love is only channeled through virtue, and the mother of the virtues is prudence, which applies universal principles to particular situations; thus prudence requires a host of virtues that only come with experience. The specific or concrete demands of love are varied, detailed, and complex. We cannot stay on that general level and reasonably expect to be able to pronounce on concrete matters bearing upon the allocation of scarce resources that have alternative uses; for that would be like attempting to drive a car through a crowded city from the perspective of a helicopter high above the city. From that height, we simply cannot see the details we'd see on the road. As a general principle, the economy ought to serve the ends of love, and no one may do evil that good may come of it, but certain economic decisions, however well motivated, end up causing higher unemployment and greater poverty, because the one making the decisions is not driving on the level of the road; the result is that he is crashing into street lamps—which he cannot see from such a high vantage point—, he is driving up onto sidewalks and has killed a few people in the process, he's failing to stop for red lights because he cannot see their color from that height, he's hit a few more pedestrians as a result, etc. There are details that can only be seen on the ground level. Indeed, the principle is always love, and the end is always human flourishing, and the helicopter pilot can help us from the angle he enjoys, for he can provide us with a general direction. But there are laws, such as speed limits which are posted on signs on the side of the road, and there are slippery road conditions that are felt on the ground. These road signs are the laws of economics, and by felt road conditions I refer to an understanding of the trade-offs involved in all our economic decisions, as well as their long term repercussions.

Philosophy and theology alone are not enough to direct the allocation of scarce resources that have alternative uses. Pope Paul VI wrote: "Too often Christians attracted by socialism tend to idealize it in terms which, apart from anything else, are very general: a will for justice, solidarity and equality. They refuse to recognize the limitations of the historical socialist movements, which remains conditioned by the ideologies from which they originated."[18]

Imagine if we were to decide that since John needs a new liver, you, Matthew, are going to give him your liver, that is, we are going to take your liver and give it to him. Why? Because human life is a basic intelligible human good, and each person has a right to live, and you have an obligation to help preserve human life." All this is true; the problem is that an important science is overlooked, one that allows us to see that this decision is a trade off, **not a solution**, namely, the science of biology. If you take Matthew's liver, he'll die. And if we take Bob's liver to save Matthew, Bob will die, and so on and so forth. When we move from general philosophical principles about human nature and what is generally good for man, to the concrete level of economic transactions without a knowledge of the laws governing these transactions, we end up causing, albeit unwittingly, a great deal of suffering by lowering a society's standard of living. Pope Leo XIII said:

> If I were to pronounce on any single matter of a prevailing economic problem, I should be interfering with the freedom of men to work out their own affairs. Certain cases must be solved in the domain of facts, case by case as they occur....Men must realize in deeds those things, the principles of which have been placed beyond dispute...These things one must leave to the solution of time and experience.[19]

The reason why the study of economics is so important is not so that we might learn to entrust economic decisions to the specialists or experts in government. Rather, it is to appreciate the vast complexities of things like market activity coordinated by prices—activity that exceeds the capacity of any bureaucracy to govern efficiently; a fact that economists are well aware of—, as well to learn to think ahead to the long term repercussions of the imposition of price controls, high corporate taxes, zoning laws, etc., and how these affect the poor.[20] It is the economically illiterate, eager to pronounce on economic matters, who are the most dangerous, whether they are in government or not; for they very often lack a healthy sense of their own limits and the limitations of human intelligence in general.

We can detect, underneath the ideological conflicts in modern politics, two visions of man that are at opposite ends of a continuum. Firstly, for a Catholic, the state is not supreme (God alone is supreme), and the role of government is to establish and maintain the entire set of conditions that will enable the members of the civil community to attain for themselves their own fullness of being. Individual persons have moral responsibilities; it is the duty of the person to cultivate the virtues, to establish community (the fundamental unit of which is the family), to fulfill his obligations towards individual persons in his vicinity as well as towards the civil community as a whole, to do his part in creating wealth, etc. But man has a propensity to sin and self-seeking; in other words, he carries the wounds of Original Sin. Thus, he needs both economic and legal incentives and constraints—without them, only a few would succeed in not destroying themselves. Most importantly, human intelligence participates in the limitations of sense perception; thus, the human person needs input from others, especially from those who are wiser and who have lived longer—for each one of us only sees things from a certain angle and acquires understanding gradually. We have a need for others to help complete our insights. Man is a historical entity, and the others he needs to complete him include, above all, those who are no longer with us, but who have left us a heritage, a tradition that was the fruit of a complex historical process too vast for us to trace in all its details. We cannot hope to surpass their intellectual and cultural achievements without years of trying to appropriate the wisdom and experience they've left us in the shape of a heritage (the institutions, laws and customs, etc.) that is much larger than we are. It is only towards the very end of our lives that we can hope to contribute anything original to this vast inheritance.

At the other extreme is a very different vision. The state is the locus of moral responsibility, and there is no natural moral law; rather, the state is the measure of what is true and right. Man is naturally good (there is no Original Sin or the propensity to self-seeking); it is institutions that corrupt him (civilization corrupts).

Thus, the solutions to our problems have to do with abolishing or radically changing these institutions. In this view, there is a strict separation between rationality and sensation—at least historically (Descartes); thus, rationality does not participate in the limitations of sense perception, and so there are clear and distinct solutions (not trade-offs) to social and economic problems that have resulted from unenlightened decisions which are now obsolete—they are unenlightened primarily because they occurred in the past. Thus, a university educated man and other intellectual elites do not require input from those who have less education; the latter only need allow themselves to be led by the former. The ordinary individual is not primarily a moral agent with responsibilities (enlightened surrogate decision makers answer to that description), but he is nonetheless the subject of rights and entitlements.[21]

The vision of man behind a political conflict today can usually be located somewhere along the line of this continuum.

The principle of subsidiarity is a very important principle of Catholic teaching, and one could say that the principle is rooted in an appreciation of the limitations of human intelligence, including the intelligence of those in public office, the university educated, intellectuals, etc. Pope Pius XI writes: "…that most weighty principle, which cannot be set aside or changed, remains fixed and unshaken in social philosophy: Just as it is gravely wrong to take from individuals what they can accomplish by their own initiative and industry and give it to the community, so also it is an injustice and at the same time a grave evil and disturbance of right order to assign to a greater and higher association what lesser and subordinate organizations can do. For every social activity ought of its very nature to furnish help to the members of the body social, and never destroy and absorb them."[22]

Many of the government interventions in Western countries, upon so many areas of the life of the community, are rooted in the latter vision of man which fails to take seriously the limitations of human intelligence and their real implications in the areas of law, education, and economics, to name only three. In *Centesimus Annus,* Pope John Paul II wrote:

In recent years the range of such intervention has vastly expanded to the point of creating a new type of state, the so-called welfare state. This has happened in some countries in order to respond better to many needs and demands, by remedying forms of poverty and deprivation unworthy of the human person. However, excesses and abuses, especially in recent years, have provoked very harsh criticisms of the welfare state, dubbed the 'social assistance state.' Malfunctions and defects in the social assistance state are the result of an inadequate understanding of the tasks proper to the state. Here again the principle of subsidiarity must be respected: A community of a higher order should not interfere in the internal life of a community of a lower order, depriving the latter of its functions, but rather should support it in case of need and help to coordinate its activity with the activities of the rest of society, always with a view to the common good.

By intervening directly and depriving society of its responsibility, the social assistance state leads to a loss of human energies and an inordinate increase of public agencies which are dominated more by bureaucratic ways of thinking than by concern for serving their clients and which are accompanied by an enormous increase in spending. In fact, it would appear that needs are best understood and satisfied by people who are closest to them and who act as neighbors to those in need. It should be added that certain kinds of demands often call for a response which is not simply material, but which is capable of perceiving the deeper human need. One thinks of the condition of refugees, immigrants, the elderly, the sick and all those in circumstances which call for assistance such as drug abusers: All these people can be helped effectively only by those who offer them genuine fraternal support, in addition to the necessary care.[23]

In the area of education, the Church has always taught that parents are the primary educators of their children, not government bureaucrats, and that schools are there to assist parents; for parents know the needs of their children. Granted, there are some parents who may lack good common sense, but these are not the people we want making decisions for us, which is why decision making power ought to be as spread out and scattered as possible, to safeguard human freedom, and to create incentives for educators and impose constraints. Government controlled education systems, it can be argued, are costly and inefficient, and very often government decisions that impose the latest and most fashionable ideas of the educational elites come in conflict with the common sense wishes and wisdom of ordinary parents.

Hidden behind this top down approach is a vision of the human person that is at odds with a Catholic understanding of the human person as a psychosomatic unity, profoundly limited by matter, a historical and personal entity who is the locus of moral responsibility. No matter how much education a person has, the gap between him and the uneducated is ultimately not very large—despite the magnified view some intellectuals might have of themselves. Although many of my former students, for example, who have taken Open level courses, will never write beyond a grade three level nor ever hope to graduate from university, they have always tended to exhibit greater wisdom and moral insight than many of the more academically brilliant ones in my university designated courses. And many patients suffering from mental illness that I've visited over the years, and who have never taken a theology course in their lives, possess spiritual insights that took me more than 30 years of studying and living the faith to acquire.

Socrates was well aware of such ironies. In *The Apology*, Socrates addresses the court:

I am only too conscious that I have no claim to wisdom, great or small. So what can he mean by asserting that I am the wisest man in the world? He cannot be telling a lie; that would not be right for him.

After puzzling about it for some time, I set myself at last with considerable reluctance to check the truth of it in the following way. I went to interview a man with a high reputation for wisdom, because I felt that here if anywhere I should succeed in disproving the oracle and pointing out to my divine authority, You said that I was the wisest of men, but here is a man who is wiser than I am.

Well, I gave a thorough examination to this person—I need not mention his name, but it was one of our politicians that I was studying when I had this experience—and in conversation with him I formed the impression that although in many people's opinion, and especially in his own, he appeared to be wise, in fact he was not. Then when I began to try to show him that he only thought he was wise and was not really so, my efforts were resented both by him and by many of the other people present. However, I reflected as I walked away, Well, I am certainly wiser than this man. It is only too likely that neither of us has any knowledge to boast of, but he thinks that he knows something which he does not know, whereas I am quite conscious of my ignorance. At any rate it seems that I am wiser than he is

to this small extent, that I do not think that I know what
I do not know.

After this I went on to interview a man with an even
greater reputation for wisdom, and I formed the same
impression again, and here too I incurred the resentment
of the man himself and a number of others.

From that time on I interviewed one person after
another. I realized with distress and alarm that I was
making myself unpopular, but I felt compelled to put my
religious duty first. Since I was trying to find out the
meaning of the oracle, I was bound to interview
everyone who had a reputation for knowledge. And by
dog, gentlemen, for I must be frank with you, my honest
impression was this. It seemed to me, as I pursued my
investigation at the god's command, that the people with
the greatest reputations were almost entirely deficient,
while others who were supposed to be their inferiors
were much better qualified in practical intelligence.[24]

Chapter 9: Father, Son, and Holy Spirit: An Exposition on the Trinity

The central mystery of the Christian faith is that God is three Persons in one divine nature. This is the mystery of the Trinity. A Christian is one who believes that God is this Trinity of Persons. The reason is that Christ revealed God as Father, Son, and Holy Spirit, and a Christian is one who believes in the claims of Christ.

Consider the following passages from the New Testament. In the Gospel of Matthew, Jesus says: "Everything has been entrusted to me by my Father, and no one knows the Son except the Father, just as no one knows the Father except the Son and those to whom the Son chooses to reveal him" (11, 27). Here Jesus reveals himself as the Son of the Father who has entrusted "everything" to him. No human being has ever made such a claim, nor could any mere human person make such a claim without a diagnosis of mental illness.

But this is not the only place in which Jesus reveals himself as the Son of the Father. Consider the Gospel of John: "The Father loves the Son and has entrusted everything to his hands" (3, 35). Later on we read: "...whatever the Father does the Son does too. For the Father loves the Son and shows him everything he himself does" (5, 21). Further, he says: "Anyone who has seen me has seen the Father, so how can you say, "Show us the Father?" (14, 9). But Jesus also reveals God as Holy Spirit, who is distinct from the Father and the Son: "I have said these things to you while still with you; but the Paraclete, the Holy Spirit, whom the Father will send in my name, will teach you everything and remind you of all I have said to you" (14, 25-26). Two chapters later, Jesus tells his disciples: "...unless I go, the Paraclete will not come to you; but if I go, I will send him to you....when the Spirit of truth comes he will lead you to the complete truth, since he will not be speaking

117

of his own accord, but will say only what he has been told; and he will reveal to you the things to come" (16, 7, 13). And after his resurrection, "he breathed on them and said: Receive the Holy Spirit. If you forgive anyone's sins, they are forgiven; if you retain anyone's sins, they are retained" (20, 22). Also, Christ commissioned his Apostles to go out and make disciples of all nations and to "baptize them in the name of the Father and of the Son and of the Holy Spirit" (Mt 28, 19).

To be a son is to have a relation to someone, namely a father. To be a father is to have a relation to an offspring. Paternity and sonship are relations. But a son is of the same nature as his father. And so if Jesus is truly the Son of God the Father, then he is of the same nature as God. In other words, Christ has a divine nature. And if only God can forgive sins, and it is through the Holy Spirit that sins are forgiven, then the Holy Spirit has a divine nature. And if baptism is carried out not only in the Father's name, but in the name of the Son, and in the name of the Holy Spirit, then all three are equal in dignity. Hence, God the Father, God the Son, and God the Holy Spirit. Not three gods, but one God.

But is this reasonable? Is it not irrational to assert that God is three distinct Persons, and at the same time assert that there is only one God? Are we not violating the principle of non-contradiction in doing so? The answer to these questions is simply, no. The rest of this article is nothing more than an attempt to summarize points made in previous centuries that show that what Christians believe about the Trinity is not irrational or impossible, but perfectly in accordance with reason. Now, it is impossible to attain a knowledge of the Trinity by means of natural reason alone. The Trinity is an article of faith that exceeds reason's natural capacity. But reason can go a long way in resolving what appear to be contradictions and inconsistencies in the doctrine.25

Reason can attain an indirect knowledge of God as First Cause of all that has being. And through a kind of negative method of reasoning, we can deduce a great deal about the divine essence. But reason cannot go so far as to attain the three Persons. Once the Trinity is a given, however, reason aided by faith can demonstrate that such a doctrine is neither absurd nor impossible. But before we begin, let us review some of what reason, unaided by faith, can attain to in the knowledge of the nature of God.

God as Ipsum Esse Subsistens

In philosophy, we speak of a thing having a certain "essence". The essence of a thing answers the question: "What is it?" It describes "what" a thing is and is expressed by the definition. What are you? The answer is, human. And a human being is a rational animal; that is "what" you are. But existence *(esse)* is not what you are, but rather is that which you "have". You are human, but you have existence (being). No created thing is its existence. Rather, it is what it is. The cow in the barn is bovine (essence), but it has existence; the dog in the park is canine (essence), but it has existence.

God, on the other hand, does **not** have a *received* act of existence, like you and me and everything else. If He did, He would not be God, but a creature, a created being. Rather, God **is** His act of existing (esse). In other words, His essence is to exist. God is pure act of existing (Ipsum Esse Subsistens).

Now anything that belongs to a thing's essence belongs to it necessarily. For example, man is essentially a rational animal. Thus, we can say that it is necessarily the case that if there is a man on the other side of this wall, he or she is rational. But whatever is outside the

119

essence of a thing does not belong to the thing necessarily, but contingently. Thus, since blond and blue eyed do not belong to the essence of man—otherwise all men would be blond and blue eyed—, the man on the other side of this wall is not necessarily blond and blue eyed; he or she might be, but is not necessarily. It is contingent upon whether or not he or she inherited these traits from his/her parents.

That is why all created things are contingent beings, and not necessary beings. Existence is not what we are, but that which we have. The act of existing is not part of man's nature; in other words, essence and existence are really distinct in creatures. For whatever belongs to a thing's nature or essence belongs to it necessarily, so if existence belongs to you essentially, then it belongs to you necessarily. That would mean that you necessarily exist, and could not **not** exist, and thus you always existed. But you and I did not always exist. We are aware that we came into existence in time and enjoy a received existence.

It follows that since God's essence is to be (to exist), God necessarily exists and cannot not exist, and thus always existed. Saying this does not constitute a proof of God's existence. To do that, we'd have to take a slightly different route, which we need not go into at this point. But once it has been established through reason that contingent beings depend upon a non-contingent being (a necessary being) in order to first exist and continue to be sustained in existence, reason can then deduce a number of things about this non-contingent being (God).

The first thing we can deduce is that God is eternal and thus never had a beginning. We can also deduce that there can only be one being whose essence is to exist, not more than one; for what would distinguish two beings who are Being Itself? It would have to be something outside of what they are in common. What are they in common? Being Itself. What is it that is outside of being? Non-being, or, in other words, nothing. Hence, nothing distinguishes them. And so there are not two non-contingent beings, but only one.

We also know that since God is pure Act of Being (Esse), He has no potentiality; and since change is the fulfillment of what exists potentially, God is unchanging. It follows from this that God is immaterial; for it is by virtue of matter that material beings are mutable, and, ultimately, matter is nothing other than potentiality. Also, if there is no potentiality in God, that means that God is not open to further perfection. God is thus perfect. And if He is perfect, all existing perfections found in creatures exist in God preeminently. And since intelligence is the highest perfection in man, God cannot lack intelligence.

Now, any perfection that exists in God will be identical to his act of existence. The reason is that there is no potentiality in God, and so He cannot be related to one of His perfections as potency is related to act, as we are related to our perfections. For example, a student is potentially a medical doctor, but when he acquires the quality of the art of medicine, he is then actually a doctor (he has a received perfection or quality). But God is *Ipsum Esse Subsistens*, without any admixture of potentiality. And so whatever perfection exists in God, it is identical to His *Esse*. It follows that God is absolutely simple, that is, He is entirely without composition. Consider the human person for a moment; we are related to our knowledge as potentiality is related to actuality. Before we acquire knowledge, we are in potentiality towards actually attaining it. After acquiring it, we are no longer in potentiality to having it, but actually have it. Nevertheless, this knowledge is a received knowledge, a received perfection. We are related to what we know as potentiality is related to actuality.

But as we said, there is no potentiality in God. Thus, His knowledge is His act of existing. He does not have knowledge; He is His knowledge. And since He is His knowledge, and He is perfect, His knowledge is perfect, which is to say He is omniscient. It also follows that since He is His knowledge, and He is First Cause of all that is, His knowledge is the cause of what is. In our case, knowledge is not the cause of the being of other things.

God is also the supreme Good. For the good is the object of desire. Now all things desire first and foremost their own perfection. But perfection (from the Latin "made through") is an actuality or act. But being is act (*esse* is the act of being). To say that all things desire first and foremost their own perfection is to say that all things desire to be, and to be most fully. Thus, "good" is a property of being. Whatever is, is good insofar as it is—evil is a privation of being. Now if God is pure Act of Being (*Ipsum Esse*) without in any way being limited by potentiality, and if good is a property of being, then God is the supreme and unlimited Good.

God knows Himself, since God is pure Act of Being, and a thing is knowable insofar as it is in act,[26] He knows Himself to be supremely and perfectly good. As the supreme and perfect Good, He rests in the possession of Himself. Hence, there is will (volition) in God; for the will is the intellectual appetite that desires and rests in the possession of the known good. Moreover, His will is identical to his act of existing, since there is no composition in God. Thus, God does not have love, rather He is His love. And since He is First Cause of all that is, His love is the cause of what is. And since love is not love unless it is freely given, God does not create by necessity. Rather, creation is free and gratuitous.

And since His intellect is His act of existing, and His will is His act of existing, and His act of existing is one,

God knows and loves Himself and all things through one act of the intellect and will, not by many different acts, as is the case with us.

Finally, to say that God is Being is not to say that all existing things are divine in some way. It is impossible to share in the act of existing of any other being. For being is not a genus, like "animal". Animal, or plane figure, or thing, are examples of a genus. Note that the genus is specified by a specific difference that is outside of it, as the genus animal is specified by "rational" to give us the species "man", or as plane figure is specified by the specific difference "three sided" to give us the species "triangle". Being cannot be a genus because there is nothing outside of it to specify it (outside of being is "non-being"). That is why being is not common, that is, it is not generic. Being is diverse, and diverse things share nothing in common. Participating in the act of existing of anything would make us one being with that thing. Yet it is this natural tendency to regard being as a universal (a genus) that is responsible for the error of pantheism—very prevalent today as it was throughout history—, which holds that God is ultimately all things.

Human reason can certainly deduce more from the notion of God as *Ipsum Esse* (Being Itself), for example, that He is the supremely beautiful and the measure of what is true. In other words, we can continue to move horizontally at this level, but this is as far as reason can go vertically, so to speak. Revelation, however, has opened up an entirely new picture that is inaccessible to unaided reason. It is as if the sky has opened, and we can reach much higher as a result. Jesus revealed God as Father, himself as the Son of the Father, and the Holy Spirit who proceeds from the Father and the Son. He has revealed that God so loved the world that He gave His only begotten Son, so that everyone who believes in him may not perish but have eternal life (Jn 3, 16).

This is a far more intimate disclosure, one that unaided reason could never have anticipated. Furthermore, human beings are called to enter into this intimate Trinitarian life. That is why there is no understanding Christianity without the doctrine of the Trinity.

But if reason cannot attain a knowledge of the Trinity, can it at least show that such a doctrine is not irrational and impossible? We would argue, yes. The rest of this chapter is devoted to doing just that.

Real Relations and the Trinity

Father and Son are terms describing persons who have a relation to one another. A relation consists in the referring of one thing to some other thing. Equality, for example, is a relation. As such, it refers one thing to another. Consider two persons of equal height. The person that is referred, namely the first person, is the subject of the relation. The person to which it is referred—in this case the second person, is called the term. The cause of the relation, in our example, the height in which the coincidence takes place, is called the ground of the relation.

A relation is either real or logical. For example, John is really the same height as Bill, and this can of soda really has the same amount of fluid as that can of soda. Equality in these cases are real relations that exist independently of the mind.

But a logical relation comes into being only in and through the activity of the intellect. Left and right in a stone, for example, are not real relations, but logical relations. They do not correspond to any real disposition in the stone, but exist only in the mind of one who apprehends the stone as right or left, because it is to the left or right of some other thing, for example the dog or cow. So too, the relation of the word "computer" to a particular device that processes information at high speeds is found neither in the word nor in the object signified. It is found only in the minds of people who have made the word stand for the computing device.

We bring up this distinction in order to point out that in God, Father, Son, and Holy Spirit are real relations, **not** logical ones, as some have maintained, such as Sabellius, an early third century heretic who argued that Father, Son and Spirit are only nominally distinct. In other words, Father, Son, and Holy Spirit are not logical relations set up by man as a way of describing how the one God relates to human beings, for example, in three different ways. Rather, it can be said that if no human or angelic persons existed, God would still be Father, Son, and Holy Spirit, three distinct Persons in one divine nature. As we say in the Creed of St. Athanasius: "We adore one God in the Trinity and the Trinity in one God, without confusing the Persons or dividing the substance of God. For the Person of the Father is different from the Person of the Son. And both are different from the Person of the Holy Spirit".

What does it mean to be a father of a son? To be a father is to be the *origin of a generation*, in this case the generation of a son. A father generates a son. A son is someone who is generated by his father and is of the same nature as his father. Christ has revealed that in God, there is a generation, for he reveals himself as Son (the generated) of the Father.

This generation, however, is **not** a physical generation. The reason is that God is not physical. Nor is this generation one that involves change, that is, the fulfillment of what exists potentially; for there is no potentiality in God, thus no change. This generation of the Son from the Father, therefore, is eternally active, that is, it is an eternal generation that does not involve movement. How then, are we to begin to understand

125

this? Both St. Augustine and St. Thomas Aquinas look to man's intellectual nature in order to come to some understanding of generation and procession in the Trinity. This is appropriate seeing that God created man in the image of Himself: "Let us make man in our image, according to our likeness" (Gn 1, 26). Man exists in the image of His knowledge and love, that is, he is like God in his capacity to know and will. When we look to our intellectual nature, we find that there is generation and conception, but of a spiritual or intellectual kind.27

The Generation of the Word

We speak of concepts. A concept is an intellectual conception. Having a concept means having conceived an idea which has a likeness to the thing known. When we know an object, there is a sense in which the object exists in us, but in an immaterial way. If we know the object, we have apprehended its nature. The essence of the tree, for example, exists outside the mind as a real existing nature. But when I know it, that is, when I apprehend "what" the tree is, the "what" (essence) of the tree is in me, which is why the knowledge I have of the tree is in me. In other words, the essence of the tree exists in a new way in me. It has a logical existence in the mind. It exists as universal, separated from its individuating conditions surrounding it in the phantasm (image).

But what I know in knowing the object is the object itself, not the idea. The idea is *that through which* I know the object. The intellect conceives this mental word or concept through which I know the thing itself outside the mind. This interior conception or mental word is a formal sign. Now to understand what is meant by formal sign, let us treat first what it is not. Consider the conventional sign, such as a wedding ring, a mathematical symbol like the plus or minus sign, or a stop sign. A wedding ring has come to signify marriage, but only by convention, that is, by general agreement. That is why one has to be taught what conventional signs mean or signify. The significance of a natural sign, on the other hand, is naturally understood. Smoke is a natural sign of fire, a scream is a natural sign of pain, and laughter is a natural sign of joy. No one had to decide and agree that smoke would signify fire, nor was it necessary to learn the signification of laughter. They are naturally known. But a formal sign is something else entirely. A formal sign is a pure sign, that is, a sign *whose sole function is to signify*. Smoke is not a formal sign because smoke is precisely what we focus our attention on first; for I know there is fire because I see smoke. But a formal sign does not call attention to itself first. Rather, it immediately signifies something other than itself. A concept is an example of a formal sign.

A concept is a conception. This kinship between knowledge and birth evident in the word "conception" is reflected in various languages. The French word *connaitre*, to know, contains in itself the verb *naitre*, to be born. The Latin *cognosco* (cognition) contains *nascor*, to be born. So too, the Greek *gignosko*, is related to *gignomai* (to be born). We see this in the Italian *conoscere*, which is related to *nascere*, also 'to be born'. We speak of generating ideas or thoughts in our students. The word generate is derived from the Latin *genus* and the Greek *genos* (kind, essence), both derived from the Aryan *gen*, to beget or engender. The same word *gen* gave rise to the old English word *kin* (next of kin, offspring, family), which in turn is reflected in the german *kennan*, to know.[28]

What revelation has made known to us is that in God there is an eternal generation of a Word: "In the beginning was the Word: the Word was with God and the Word was God. He was with God in the beginning. Through him all things came into being, not one thing came into being except through him" (Jn 1, 1-3). The Word (Logos) is distinct from his origin ("with God"), but the "Word was God". We know that the Word is the Son and his origin is the Father: "The Word became flesh, he lived among us, and we saw his glory, the glory that he has from the Father as only Son of the Father, full of grace and truth" (Jn 1, 14).

This generation is like the generation of the word by the intellect, but it is unlike it in that the interior word conceived by the human intellect is **not** a person. It is also unlike the divine generation in that the generation of the interior word by the intellect is a type of change; the mind is moved from potential understanding to actual understanding. But there is no change in God, for He is pure act of existing. If the Word is God, then the Word is pure and eternal actuality, eternally generated.

The human generation of a son is like the divine generation of the Son in that what is generated is not merely a concept but a Person. It is also like the divine generation in that the son who is generated is of the same nature as the father. It is unlike the divine generation in that the person generated (the human son) is a distinct being from the father. In God, the generated Son is of the same nature as the Father. But God's nature is His act of existing, and so God the Father and God the Son are not two beings, but one in being

The Son is generated from the Father as His eternal Word. Consider that the interior word conceived by the human intellect is the essence of the thing known. The essence of a material thing is existentially neutral. It can exist outside the mind as an existing nature, and it can simultaneously exist inside the mind, having a logical or intentional existence. And yet the essence itself really is inside the mind, which is why through it I really know the nature of the object outside my mind. Its nature is in me immaterially; my potential intellect has become what it knows immaterially. Hence, there is a likeness between the interior word (my concept of the tree) and the object known through it (the tree outside my mind). This is a more perfect likeness than that of an image reflected in a mirror and the thing of which the image is a reflection.

Similarly, the likeness between the Word and the Father is more perfect than that of the interior word and the object known. The reason is that the interior word exists differently in me than it does outside me (it exists in me immaterially, and outside of me materially). But the likeness between the Word and the Father is perfect—for the Word is one in being with the Father.

Just as it is through the interior word conceived in the mind that we know the thing outside the mind, it is through the Word that the Father knows Himself perfectly, because the Word is the perfect image of the Father. The Word is His eternal and perfect self-understanding. The Word is the perfect expression, the perfect likeness of the Father, which would not be the case were he separated from the Father or created by the Father. And yet the Son is related to the Father as generated, and the Father is related to the Son as origin.

Now relation is one of the nine accidents of material substance (quantity, quality, where, when, relation, action, passion, posture, habit). But there are no accidents in God; for He is not subject any accidental mode of being, otherwise He'd be related to it as potency is related to act, which is impossible, since He is pure Act of Being. Therefore, any real relation in God is identical to His Act of Being. This means that any real relation that exists in God is subsistent. This means that it is a Person, for God's nature is intelligent; thus, He is a Person (a person is an individual substance of a rational nature). And so paternity in God is a Person, and filiation in God is a Person.[29] As was said above, these

129

are real relations, not logical relations. The Father is really distinct from the Son because paternity and filiation are really distinct and opposite relations. And if these relations, which are opposite and distinct, are Persons, then it follows that Father and Son are really distinct Persons, yet of the same nature. In God, these distinct and opposite relations are divine and subsistent Persons.

The Procession of Love

Now the Father not only knows Himself through the Son, his Word, but the Father loves what He knows; for what He knows is supremely good and infinitely lovable. In other words, the Father loves the Son. He loves the Son with infinite and omnipotent love. The Son, who is distinct from the Father and eternally begotten of the Father, loves the Father with infinite and boundless love. The mutual love between the Father and the Son is subsistent and personal, for whatever is in God is identical to His act of existing. The love between a human father and his son is unlike the love between God the Father and God the Son in that the mutual love between them is not a subsistent person; but the love between the Father and the Son is a third Person, namely the Holy Spirit.

It is a third Person because the procession of love is different than the generation of a word.[30] But there are no terms for what comes forth by love and the relation that results from it.[31] But the relation of the principle of what comes forth by love is called *spiration* or breathing. The answering relation is called a proceeding forth or procession. The Holy Spirit is this procession. And since love follows upon knowledge, the procession originates in the Father and the Son, not in the Father alone, as does the Son's generation. This spiration is thus a common spiration.[32]

130

The love that the Father has for the Son is not the Word; It is the love He has for His Word, His only begotten Son. The love that the Son has for the Father is not the Father. The Father is the object of His love. But this love, which is neither the Father nor the Son, exists in God, and whatever exists in God is God (identical to His act of existing). Thus, the mutual love of the Father and the Son is a divine Person, a real relation different than filiation. For the Son proceeds from the Father as Word, but the Holy Spirit proceeds from the Father and the Son *as Love*. Hence, The Creed of St. Athanasius:

> The Father was made by no one: neither created nor generated. The Son is from the Father: not created, but generated. The Holy Spirit is from the Father and the Son: not made, not created, not generated, but proceeding. There is one Father, therefore, not three fathers. And there is one Son, not three sons. And there is one Holy Spirit, not three spirits.

The Trinity and the Nature of Charity: A Summary of Richard of St. Victor

To love is to will good, either for oneself or for another. It also includes resting in the possession of the good. The object of the will is the good, and so the will naturally loves the good. But a person of intelligence and will does not necessarily choose what is best for himself, nor does he necessarily will the good of another. His love—either for himself or for another—may be deficient. But the greatest achievement of love is to love other human persons as another self. The perfection of this kind of love is supernatural charity (caritas).

Because I can know the other person as another self, for example, that he is of the same nature as myself, that he is a person who also naturally seeks his own

131

perfection, etc., I have the ability to will what is best for him as another self. I am not bound by nature to pursue my own good to the exclusion of the good of another. I necessarily will my own happiness, but a genuine love for another will mean that I wish happiness befall him or her. But if my understanding of what constitutes happiness is distorted, so too my love for myself and for others will suffer from that distortion. A rightly ordered love prefers the greater good to the lesser good. The greatest love wills that the other enjoy the greatest good, and thus the greatest possible happiness; it wills that the happiness of knowing and loving God befall another.

This most selfless of loves involves a kind of exit-of-self, or an ability to become another. In love, I wish that the other be more fully. I will good for him not for my sake, but for his sake. Thus, when I know another person, he exists in me as known; but when I love another person, I exist outside myself as him, willing that he possess and delight in the good. And so love, above all things, enlarges the human person. Loving the other as another self expands us beyond ourselves such that his good becomes my good, and his joy becomes my joy. We are always finite, but as we grow in love, we become larger and increasingly like God, who is boundlessly large, but without size. By growing in love, we can forever approach a likeness to God.

But the one who will not love the other as another self, but only as a means to himself, does not expand and enlarge but contracts or shrinks. He is an egoist who remains small and at the very center of his world.[33] But genuine love is expansive. It longs to share its own happiness with another. There is nothing better than to love God under the aspect of friendship and wish that others benefit equally from such a friendship. In other words, there is nothing better than charity.

Now, we know through reason that God is perfect and supremely good. If God is perfectly good, and there is nothing more perfect than charity, then there is charity or perfect love in God. In fact, we can say that God is Love (1 Jn 4, 8), since whatever exists in God is identical to his Act of Being.

But no one can be said to have charity on the basis of his own private love of himself. It follows that where there is a plurality of persons lacking, charity does not and cannot exist. Hence, there must be a plurality of persons in God.34

We might raise an objection at this point, namely, that this does not show that in God there is a plurality of persons, but merely that creation exists as the object of divine charity. But this does not work. For it would imply that God is not sufficient unto Himself and thus needs to create in order to acquire the perfection of charity. Nor is creation sufficient, because creation cannot have any perfection that it does not receive from God. Thus, the idea that God would create something in order to acquire something for Himself is impossible.

Also, God cannot have a supreme charity for a created person, because such a love is disordered. To draw a simple analogy, consider a person who loves his pet rock like he should love his own child. He sleeps with it, eats with it, waters it, registers it for school, etc. Such a love is disordered, for it is not proportionate to the nature of a rock. Some people have such a disordered love for animals, in particular those who hold that non-rational animals have an inalienable right to live and not be slaughtered to serve the needs of man. Such love is not proportionate to the nature of the animal, which in this case is loved as a human person ought to be loved, that is, as an end in itself.

So too in God, charity would be disordered if He loves supremely someone who should not be supremely loved—and only God should be supremely loved. Now if God is supremely good, He is supreme Love, and the perfection of love requires a plurality of persons. For as long as anyone loves no one else as much as he loves himself, he has not reached the perfection of charity, and if God loves no one else as much as he loves himself, he has not the supreme level of charity, which is to love supremely someone who ought to be loved supremely, namely someone of the same nature as God.

Moreover, nothing is more pleasing than charity. The more we learn to love another as another self and grow in that love, the larger we become—for I begin to exist as him, and as her, and whoever else I choose to love. In other words, I begin to exist more fully. But happiness is fullness of being. Thus, the more I will that others share equally in the good that I love, the happier I become. As he begins to possess and enjoy that good, I rejoice because I have begun to exist as him. Through this transportation of love, his good has become my good.

God cannot but possess a perfect and supreme happiness that suffers no deficiency, because he is the supreme good. Now, it is impossible that there be lacking in God either one who can show charity or one to whom charity can be shown; for there are a plurality of Persons in God. And it is characteristic of love to wish to be loved much by the one you love much. It follows that love cannot be entirely pleasing if it is not mutual. But in mutual love, it is necessary that there be one who gives love and one who returns love. Thus, if God is supremely happy, there must exist in God a mutual exchange of love between Persons of the same nature.

Richard also confirms his conclusions by focusing on the fullness of divine glory. What is more glorious, he asks, and what is more magnificent than to have nothing that one does not want to share? In God, there can be no miserly holding back or inordinate squandering. The fullness of glory requires that there be not lacking a sharer of glory. And if this is what God wills, it cannot but be the case, since God is omnipotent. And if His omnipotent will is unchangeable, He has willed a sharer in His glory for all eternity. Thus, it is necessary that an eternal Person have a coeternal Person who eternally shares in the fullness of the divine glory.

And of course supreme charity demands equality of persons. The nature of love is such that it is not sufficient if the one being loved supremely does not return supreme love. A love received that is not returned is dead, as a seed that is sown but does not bear fruit is dead. But to return supreme love requires one equal in supremacy.

But love not only demands a plurality of persons. It demands no less than three persons. All this is implied in what we have reasoned so far. My very existence is a gift; it is a sharing in the goodness of being. As a human person, I share in being more profoundly than does a brute animal. And yet my existence is understood by me to be received. A gift given gratuitously and received has love at its origin; for to love is to will and impart to another what is good. If I have truly learned to love, I will choose to share the goodness that has been communicated to me, that is, to communicate it to another as much as I am able to. Hence, Richard says: "Certainly in mutual and very fervent love nothing is rarer and more magnificent than to wish that another be loved equally by the one whom you love supremely and by whom you are supremely loved"[35]

It follows that in God, the one who loves supremely and who wills to be loved supremely delights in the eternal actualization of that will, namely in the attainment of that willed love. One cannot be said to have attained the perfection of love if he cannot take pleasure in the sharing of his joy. Thus, it is a sign of tremendous weakness not to be able to allow a sharing of love and conversely, a sign of great perfection to be able to allow a sharing of love. Great it is to allow it, greater still to undertake it with rejoicing; but greatest to search for it with longing.[36]

Now in those who are mutually loved, the perfection of each requires a sharer of the love that has been shown to them; for if he does not will what perfect goodness demands, he does not achieve the fullness of goodness. But God is perfect goodness, and so the divine Persons will a sharer of the supreme love mutually received. If they will it but it cannot be done, then there is a deficiency of power in God, which is impossible.

And so the Father loves the Son supremely, and the Son receives and returns that love supremely, that is, he loves the Father in return. But in receiving that love, He wills to share it equally. The Father receives the supreme love of the Son and with a will identical and omnipotent wills to share it equally. But to have it shared equally requires a third divine Person. That love, which the Father and the Son will to share, is that Person. They will that the Person who shares in that love be the fullness of that love, of which there is nothing greater. The third Person must be worthy of supreme love, hence He must be divine, that is, one nature with the Father and the Son. Hence, the Holy Spirit is the mutual divine and personified love between the Father and the Son.

Concluding Thoughts

There is much more that can be considered and other angles from which to examine this doctrine. But if we glance at the entire hierarchy of being in the physical universe, we discern various kinds of emanation or procession at all levels of the hierarchy, and the higher up on the hierarchy, the more interior is the emanation. For example, things at the mineral level are not alive; for a living thing moves itself from within itself, but a non-living thing is moved by virtue of an extrinsic principle, for example another rock, or the wind, etc.,. And so what emanates from a moving rock is a likeness of motion, imparted to another non-living thing, or an impression left in some external thing, such as the earth. The effect has a likeness to the cause, but it is entirely external to the cause.

As we move up to the vegetative level, we discern a more interior emanation. The plant reproduces its like from within itself, but the seed of that likeness proceeds outward and into the ground, and the development and complete actualization of the offspring takes place outside the parent plant. Moreover, the process begins outside the plant with nutrition, at the level of the roots. Higher up on the scale, we notice that reproduction in some animals has become somewhat more interior. Gestation takes place within the animal. The offspring is nurtured within, but is born to exist without. But the specific emanation belonging to sentient life occurs on the level of perception—for an animal is a living sentient creature. I refer to the emanation of the percept by which the animal perceives the object outside of it, without that object or animal changing substantially. This kind of knowledge, however, is imperfect because material things are not capable of perfect self-reflection, and sensation is intimately tied up in matter; for we do not sense ourselves sensing. But in man we find the generation of the interior word by which he knows *the nature of the thing* outside of him without undergoing any substantial change and without the object of his knowledge undergoing change. The emanation of verbal communication presupposes this more interior conception. And in this kind of knowledge, unlike sense knowledge, the knower achieves total self-reflection, which is why a person knows himself knowing and sensing, and knows that he knows. In knowing himself, man's essence exists in him intentionally. Hence, he is present to himself through this word. He can talk to himself, as we often do when we are alone. And so even in us, we experience a kind of plurality that is an echo of the Trinitarian plurality.

As we climb the hierarchy of being in the physical universe, we discern that generation becomes increasingly interior, and so it is reasonable to conclude that the angelic intellect has an even greater likeness to God than does the human intellect. Angelic knowing does not begin externally, that is, with sensation, as does human knowing, but is from beginning to end entirely interior. But in God, the generation of the Word and the procession of Love are entirely interior, eternal, and existentially perfect. Thus even a bird's eye glance at the hierarchy of material being hints at what revelation fully discloses.

Our destiny, according to what has been revealed in the Person of Christ, is to enter fully into the life of the Trinity. That life begins with the life of supernatural charity. Our purpose here is to begin the process of self-expansion through the transportation made possible by supernatural charity. Everything having to do with the life of the Church is ordered to this end. In Baptism we die to our old life, which was slavery to the constriction of sin and self-negating egoism. We enter into the tomb of Christ in order to rise with him to the new life of grace, that is, to the life of faith, hope and charity, given in baptism as sheer gift. In Confirmation we are sealed with the Holy Spirit of the Father and the Son and are given the power to desire above all things that God be loved and glorified and that the blessing of salvation befall others. In the Eucharist we are given the very substance of Christ and are joined intimately to him, body, blood, soul and divinity. Matrimony is a sign of the love that Christ has for his bride, the Church, for whom he gave up his life that she might enter into the eternal life of the Trinity. The very precepts and requirements of the Christian moral life are nothing other than the full implications of the life of charity. Actions condemned by the Church are simply instances of choices that are incompatible with charity and our intratrinitarian destiny. It is not these prohibitions that limit us, but those very choices which are prohibited that enslave and destroy us.

All this, of course, needs to be explicated more fully. But it all begins and ends with the Most Holy Trinity, the Father, and the Son, and the Holy Spirit.

Chapter 10: The Humour and Playfulness of God

Often, at hockey, baseball, or football games, when the television camera is pointed at the crowd, we see someone holding up a sign on which is written: Jn 3: 16. If someone sitting in front of the television is curious enough to look it up, he will come upon the following text of Scripture: "God so loved the world that he gave his only begotten Son, so that everyone who believes in him may not perish, but have eternal life". The entire good news of the gospel is summed up in that one verse.

The Person of the Son did not come to us in anger, to condemn the world. He came to reveal the inner life of the Trinity, which is a life of absolute love between the Father and the Son. The Holy Spirit is that very love in Person.

That such a sign would appear in the context of a game, whether it be a hockey, baseball, or football game, is apt indeed, because the Incarnation of the Son and his redemption of the human race is a game, one that is sacred, serious, mysterious and full of humour. The narrative of this game, moreover, will preoccupy the blessed for an eternity.

Allow me to begin with a reflection on the divine humour. For laughter is such a mysterious phenomenon. I often wonder why certain things make us laugh. A key to unlocking the mystery of humour in order to explore it more deeply is the word itself, from the Latin *humus*, which means 'soil', 'dirt', or 'ground'. The word 'human' is also derived from *humus*; for a man is one who is 'from the ground': "Then the Lord God formed man from the dust of the ground…" (Gn 2, 6).

The word 'humility' is also derived from the Latin *humus*. A humble person is one who has not forgotten his origins, namely, his origin in God: "…the Lord God…breathed into his nostrils the breath of life; and the man became a living being" (Gn 2, 7); as well as his origin 'from the ground': "Let me take it upon myself to speak to the Lord, I who am but dust and ashes" (Gn 18, 27).

The humble man, among other things, knows he is smaller than God, entirely dependent upon him, and subject to his law, and he knows that he is weak and vulnerable to destruction like any other material thing. Moreover, he refuses to ascend to heights disproportionate to his material nature, unlike the proud man who stubbornly insists on being his own god and the measure of what is true and good; the proud have very little sense of their own limitations.

Humility is akin to humour because the more humble a person is, the more a spirit of humour permeates him, and thus the more he is able to laugh, in particular at himself. Evil has a narcissistic or egotistical character to it, and one quality that egoists lack is the ability to laugh at themselves. Those in darkness typically take themselves very seriously, but they take others, their lives and especially their salvation, very lightly; the saints, on the contrary, take themselves very lightly, but they take the souls of others very seriously.

This is so evident in the lives of the martyrs, who would often joke about themselves on their way to execution. William Roper tells of his father in law, Thomas More, who joked with the Master Lieutenant as he was being escorted up a weak scaffold: "I pray you, Master Lieutenant, see me safe up, and for my coming down let me shift for myself". With a cheerful countenance, he said to the executioner: "Pluck up thy spirits, man, and be not afraid to do thine office; my neck is very short; take heed therefore thou strike not awry, for saving of thine honesty." And yet Thomas wrote some of his best theological works while imprisoned in the Tower, evidently more concerned for the truth of Christ and the souls outside the Tower than for his own life.

Those who dwell in darkness, on the contrary, don't mind playing with people, using them, manipulating them like pawns in their own little game that has as its end the maximum level of self glorification that they can procure for themselves. Such people do not have the eyes to laugh at themselves, for they never see any incongruity between themselves and a higher law or standard that measures them, because they refuse to acknowledge and submit to any law other than their own will.

A person has to affirm a law greater and more lovely than himself in order to be able to laugh at himself, as he beholds how much he has fallen short of the standard it holds out to him. Instead, the egoist laughs at others whom he takes lightly, and he does so sardonically.

To be human is to exist at this juncture between God above and the ground below, and it is only here, suspended between heaven and earth, that genuine humour is at all possible. A person who is far too immersed in the affairs of the earth, and who loves the earth inordinately, laughs with great difficulty. He is too serious, and his mind is far too weighed down by the matter of the world to see himself and others from a distance and against the background of the divine law, which is the angle from which joyful laughter is made possible.

A person who is so elevated off the ground laughs with great difficulty as well, because he has forgotten that he is from the dirt. He is no longer aware of his fumbling nature, his limitations, and so he lives under the illusion that he is in control—and how can he laugh when he will no longer be surprised.

Humour exists in that space between heaven and earth in which one beholds the affairs of fallible, fumbling, forgetful human persons in light of the divine law. That is why the saints exhibit the greatest sense of humour.

Consider the humour in irony. The nicknames that children give to one another are often very funny, because they are full of irony. Think of Hercules, the kid so named because he couldn't lift a sack of potatoes to save his life, or the tall kid whose friends call Shorty, or the short kid they call Stretch, and the fat kid 'Slim'.

Or, think of the child that laughs at the TV when a witch turns a man into a frog, or the proud man who walks high and mighty, then suddenly slips on a banana peel, or bends over to pick up the paper and rips his pants at the seat. We laugh because we are struck by the irony, the latter a kind of reparative irony, that is, a much needed reminder that we are only matter and spirit.

When we consider these two aspects of humour, namely humility and irony, we see that God really has a great sense of humour. The Incarnation of the Son of God is a perfect blend of irony and humility.

St. Gregory of Nyssa highlights the irony in the Incarnation in his *Sermons on the Beatitudes*:

What more humble for the King of creation than to share in our poor nature? The Ruler of rulers, the Lord of lords puts on voluntarily the garb of servitude. The Judge of all things becomes a subject of governors; He who holds the universe in His hands finds no place in the inn, but is cast aside into the manger of irrational beasts. The perfectly Pure accepts the filth of human nature, and after going through all our poverty passes on to the experience of death. Look at the standard by which to measure voluntary poverty! Life tastes death; the Judge is brought to judgment, the Lord of the life of all creatures is sentenced by the judge; the King of all heavenly powers does not push aside the hands of the executioners. Take this, He says, as an example by which to measure your humility. [37]

Furthermore, God, who cannot be contained, but who contains all, chooses to remain really and truly present to us under the appearance of ordinary bread. Imagine if one were to hold up a piece of rye bread and declare out loud: "This is my uncle Joe. He promised that he would remain present to the family after his death, in this piece of bread". Turning to the rye bread he continues: "We miss you, uncle Joe. We love you! You'll always be close by, in the bread basket, and we'll greet you daily on one knee."

We'd be compelled to laugh at such a spectacle, for it is ridiculous. But God the Son has chosen to do just that, to remain substantially present to us under the appearance of ordinary and unexciting bread. The sense of ridicule is gone, because love is serious, and above all, it is true, Christ is the Bread of Life, literally. But the humour is still mystically discernible; for here is humility and irony at its best; for it is divine humour, and the joke is on those who don't believe it and who ridicule those who do. The Eucharist is the perfect example of the humility that takes itself lightly.

The Incarnation reveals not only the absolute mercy of God, and the infinite love of God, but it reveals at the same time the joyful humour of God. When we enter into the life of the Trinity by faith, we enter into God's humour.

I recall the reaction of a very gifted but quiet student of mine upon coming to understand some very profound truths on the soul, universals and the nature of knowledge in the thought of Plato. On more than one occasion, I'd look over in his direction to find him laughing by himself. I finally inquired of his laughter, and he simply pointed out: "I get it". He came to understand. Truth is beautiful, it is awe inspiring, and in his case he was moved to joyous laughter as the lofty ideas of Plato came in contact with a spirit that is united to matter. The joy and surprise of coming into the possession of what is eternally true spilled over into his body, inducing him to laugh.

And God is Truth Itself. He is subsistent Truth, just as He is subsistent Being, Goodness, and Beauty. To behold God as He is in Himself is to be possessed by Joy Itself, and a body possessed by Joy is one that is disposed to laughter.

Divine Playfulness

Not only is the mystery of humour rooted in God; so too the mystery of play. Comedy is a type of playing. A good comedian plays with his audience. He depends, however, on an audience that is willing to play along.

Creation as well as the re-creation of our redemption, is divine play; it is a sacred game. Even for us, recreation typically involves play.

To play—because it is a type of leisure—is to engage in activity not for the sake of some further end, but simply for its own sake. It is activity that is meaningful in itself. Human play involves a space in which to play, a field, and the game to be played will have an intelligible structure, with rules, boundaries, penalties for infractions, and goals. It will involve a physical and/or mental struggle to achieve the goal; one that brings rest, even when it is strenuous, for it is a leisurely and intriguing struggle.

The game—if it involves teams—aims principally at a common good, to be shared in whole and entire by every player, namely victory. But once play begins, the game cannot be controlled as a whole, but acquires a life of its own that is larger than any one individual. It is always full of surprises, which is why it is so much fun. The players become part of a kind of providence, a mini providence, without which there can be no fun, and thus no game.

145

For this reason, to control the game, such as its outcome, is to allow it to lose its hold on us, and this would drain it of its meaning. A game controlled by any one or more individuals is not a game as those playing might believe it is. Rather, it is a sham, not a playing between equals. In such a situation, the players have been lied to and reduced to pawns to serve the personal or private ends of a manipulator. So too is the audience being played. In other words, the childlike quality of the players and spectators—the quality which makes play possible—is being exploited.

Genuine play begets narrative. It is contemplative. Human persons will discuss a good play that is part of a larger game for years afterwards. Baseball's most eloquent and illustrious poet and former Commissioner, Bartlett Giomatti, writes: "..the fullest, most expansive, most public talk is the talk in the lobby, baseball's second-favorite venue. The lobby is the park of talk; it is the enclosed place where the game is truly told, because told again and again. Each time it is played and replayed in the telling, the fable is refined, the nuances burnished the color of old silver. The memories in baseball become sharpest as they recede, for the art of telling improves with age".38

Play inspires narrative because like a powerful river current, the game sweeps the observer off his feet, elevating him to a new level of participation and observation (contemplation). It is restful for both player and observer, because the game takes us out of the workaday world and into a higher order in which one is no longer conscious of the world's time that closes us in and hurries us on, but a heavenly time that does not limit, but liberates. This is especially evident in baseball, where there is no clock. The game itself has become the clock.

That is why a game, even a playing season, anticipates eternity. Bartlett Giomatti writes:

Mutability had turned the seasons and translated hope to memory once again. And, once again, she had used baseball, our best invention to stay change, to bring change on. That is why it breaks my heart, that game— not because in New York they could win because Boston lost; in that, there is a rough justice, a reminder to the Yankees of how slight and fragile are the circumstances that exalt one group of human beings over another. It breaks my heart because it was meant to, because it was meant to foster in me again the illusion that there was something abiding, some pattern and some impulse that could come together to make a reality that would resist the corrosion; and because, after it had fostered again that most hungered-for illusion, the game was meant to stop, and betray precisely what it promised....I need to think something lasts forever, and it might as well be that state of being that is a game; it might as well be that, in a green field, in the sun.[39]

Now the Wisdom of God, who is with God and who is God (Jn 1, 1), eternally plays before the face of God like a child: "When he established the heavens, I was there,...when he marked out the foundations of the earth, then I was beside him, like a little child; and I was daily his delight, making play before him always, at play in his inhabited world and delighting in the sons of men" (Prov 8, 27, 29-31).

Chokmah can be translated as wit, skillful, wisely, or wisdom. The Wisdom that 'makes play' before God is witty, wise, skillful. He is like a child, because children play. At the same time, He is like an artist who plays wittily and skillfully.

God creates through the *Logos*, His Word, who plays. In other words, God's creating is a divine playing, and creation is His divine game. Divine providence is the rhythm of that game, which exists for us who are both players and spectators in one. Creation does not proceed from God out of necessity, but out of a love that freely chooses to communicate itself and make itself visible. As the artist creates on the basis of what he sees, similarly God, who knows Himself in His Word who is Wisdom Itself, playing like a child before Him, creates according to what He sees in His Word.

And so creation reflects marvelously and of course imperfectly and in varied ways the beauty and wit of this divine playfulness of the *Logos*. To contemplate the works of the Word is to be drawn into his playing, and so it should come as no surprise that we are moved to play wittily and creatively. To behold the beauty of this world is often to be inspired to express it and imitate it in some limited way, either in song, dance, prose or verse, or on canvas, or else to enter into the beautiful works of others.

Children know naturally how to play, and they are very serious about their play. Try disrupting the play of children—i.e., take the ball and run—and we soon discover that the playful is not opposed to the serious. And children are very serious about law; for they understand that law is an integral part of play. As they gather friends to play, they immediately go about drawing boundary lines, promulgating the law, the rules, the penalties for infraction; for without law there is no playing. Law exists to make play a possibility, that is, for the sake of the freedom to play. It is ordered, intelligible, harmonious, and protective of the good, in this case, the good of the game. One cannot arbitrarily decide, after hitting the ball, to run to third then back home again. One must proceed to first base, then second, third, then home. The kid who refuses to play by the rules is not serious enough about the game. He ruins the fun for everyone.

Only those who want to play by their own rules, those who want to control the outcome of the game, see law as restrictive, burdensome, and opposed to liberty. Those who refuse to play because it isn't their game see in law a desire to dominate and control, but only because they cannot imagine the possibility that others might be radically different from themselves and are willing to submit to a higher law for the sake of being taken up into the mini providence of the game.

Man's destiny is to learn to play the Lord's game, which is a very specific game with rules, some of which are absolute, and some relative. We are invited to enter into this divine game so as to enter into the Sabbath rest of His divine and eternal playing. To learn to play is to learn to become a child again: "Truly I tell you, unless you change and become like children, you will never enter the kingdom of heaven" (Mt 18, 3). For what is it that children love to do above all things? They love to play. Without play, there is no childhood, and without a childhood, one does not know how to be an adult.

How does one play? By surrendering to divine providence, that is, by allowing oneself to be taken up into the Lord's re-creation; it is to enter into the game of grace, the Person of Christ, who descended in order to lift us up into the humour and play of the Divine Persons. His game is profoundly serious, and it is bound by strict rules and foul lines. But the latter exist for the sake of the beauty and order of the play, not to mention the good of the players.

The point of this game, like baseball, is to return home. Some of us may be called to make a sacrifice fly so that the man on third can make it home, but all of us are called ultimately to help one another home, and when the enemy takes an aggressive posture, all of us must play our positions faithfully, patiently, without changing the rules that are not ours to change.

It is possible, however, to lose our balance in one of two ways. It is not a matter of Left and Right, Conservative or Liberal; rather, it is a matter of becoming too serious, or heavy of spirit. Like those who refuse to play, we can, even while belonging to the right team, begin to take ourselves too seriously and the souls of others too lightly. Children take play and law seriously and themselves lightly, but some people who have freely entered into the play of Divine Providence become bored with childhood and delight in seeing themselves as slightly larger (inflated) than they actually are. Being an individual member of a large team is not all that flattering, and so some will experiment in ways that exceed the boundaries of the game. Inevitably, they will hide their recklessness under the guise of being light of heart. The problem is that they fail to take seriously enough what pertains to the salvation of souls.

The other extreme also involves a heavy spirit. These are serious about souls, but they as well are too serious about themselves. And so they become self-righteous, suspicious of those with whom they do not see eye to eye. And they fail to grasp the character of the game of which they are a part, that games are not, as a whole, controlled by coaches, managers, or team captains, but have a life of their own. These people are not secure in God, and so they laugh rarely.

But if we don't join this game, inevitably we join another, the game of those opposed to providence, one fast paced, unfestive, strenuous and exhausting, one in which to play is to work, ultimately for nothing. Behind this game is an empty promise of rest, and the humour that belongs to it is derisive and mocking, one that plays with reputations, soils the character, perverts the order of things, and aims to expose what it sees as the façade of moral nobility.

When the playing becomes difficult, when it rains and we are losing, we need only remember that a game is meant to be played in a spirit of joy. For we have an advantage in that we've been told and have been asked to believe that victory is guaranteed, not our own individual victory—unless we persevere—, but the victory of the team. It is right to taste the sadness of losing an inning, but we despair if we forget that the game is ours, and we have a part to play in this victory.

Chapter 11: Angels and Divine Providence

When we consider the relationship between things on the hierarchy of being within the physical universe, it appears that what is lower or inferior exists for the sake of what is higher. This does not mean that what is higher will never serve the inferior. On the contrary, a superior creature may very well serve an inferior one. But the former does not exist for the sake of the latter; rather, the latter exists for the former.

For example, within the natural hierarchy, the mineral level exists not for itself, but for the sake of things at higher levels. Vegetative life moves what exists on the mineral level in order that it may serve a higher purpose, for example, in the case of nutrition when non-living matter is sublimated by a living thing, which makes it a part of itself, changing it into living matter. Similarly, animals use plants to serve their needs. Birds build nests, beavers build dams, and animals eat plants, as well as animals of inferior strength.

Man, too, uses all the levels below him, elevating them to serve his rationally conceived ends. He uses metal to build clocks in order to keep track of time, ink and paper to express his ideas, or trees to build desks, houses, and an altar upon which to offer the sacrifice of the Mass. He makes flutes and other instruments to serve higher goods, such as the contemplation of beauty.

And man uses animals; he uses horses to pull carriages that carry newlyweds around the city, or oxen to plough his fields, and he uses various kinds of animals to feed himself. He also decorates his home with birds and fish and other living creatures.

What is particularly noteworthy in all of this is that in serving the higher, the lower levels are completely unaware of the higher purposes for which they are being employed. And yet their elevation bestows greater nobility upon them. Metal is unaware that it has become a wedding ring that symbolizes something exceedingly noble, and a horse carrying a decorated officer in a parade has no understanding of the nobler purpose it is being made to serve.

Now man is at the top of the scale of the hierarchy of being in the physical universe, but he is not at the top of the scale of the hierarchy of being. In fact, man is at the bottom of the scale of the hierarchy of intelligent creatures; out of all the intellectual creatures that God has created, man is the least intelligent.

Now it is contrary to the dignity of man to be used by his equal, that is, by another man. A very important precept of natural law is that human persons ought not to be used as a means to an end, but always as an end. To use a person is to violate the requirement to treat equals equally. But an essentially superior being, that is, one of a higher nature, can use man without violating his dignity. Just as every level of the hierarchy uses the level below it to serve the higher and in so doing elevates it, man is used by God to serve a higher purpose, one that man is only vaguely aware of. God moves human persons to serve His eternally conceived end, just as man moves lower creatures to serve his own ends.

Consider how man makes use of a number of horses to pull a royal carriage. It is man who moves these creatures, and yet these horses are real movers; for they really are pulling the carriage. They are being made to behave specifically as brute animals, but in a way that surpasses their own natural capacity; for a horse could never determine itself to do such a thing on its own, such as harness itself to a carriage or saddle itself in order to carry a police officer and then determine the best route to take.

Similarly, God moves man *as man*; He does so without violating his dignity. In fact, in being used by God, man is elevated to serve a higher end that ennobles him. God moves the human person without violating

153

his free-will, just as man uses a brute without violating the specific powers of its nature.40 No matter what course of action man freely chooses, his entire life, including his free choices, is part of a larger order and is made to serve an end that is outside his limited purview. Jean Pierre de Caussade writes:

The Holy Spirit, with his own action for pen, writes a living gospel, but it will not be readable until the day of glory when it will be taken out of the printing press of this life and published. What a beautiful history! What a fine book the Holy Spirit is writing now! The book is in the press, there is no day on which the letters which make it up are not being composed, on which the ink is not applied and the sheets printed. But we dwell in the night of faith; the paper is blacker than the ink, the characters are all in confusion, the language is not of this world, nothing can be understood of it. You will be able to read this book only in heaven. If we could see the life of God and could contemplate all creatures, not in themselves, but in their principle, if we could also see the life of God in all objects, how his divine action moves them, mingles them, assembles them, opposes them to each other, pushes them all to the same point by diverse means, we should recognize that all things in this divine work have their reasons, their scale of measurement, their mutual relations. But how read this book the characters of which are unknown, vast in number, upside down and blotted with ink? If the blending of twenty-six letters results in such incomprehensible diversity that they suffice to compose an infinite number of different volumes, all admirable, who can express what God is doing in the universe?41

Angels and Providence

154

But God uses secondary causes to move human persons for the same reason that He uses human secondary causes to move the mineral, vegetative, and animal levels. That is why angels are the special instruments of His providence with respect to human beings. Angels are not subject to the requirement to treat human persons in a way that respects their status as equal in dignity, because angels are not our equals, and so they need not treat us as such.

Moreover, angels use man without violating his freedom, that is, they use him within the context of his own free will. This could not happen if an angel was man's equal and subject to the limits of matter. This does not mean, however, that human persons know they are part of a larger order or that they must consent to being so ordered. At most, the human person can become aware of the higher order of divine providence through reason illuminated by faith, but he cannot know the details of that order in all their significance until he sees God as He is in Himself. Human beings have about as much knowledge of the plan they are made to serve as a horse has of our own plans of which the horse is made a part.

Angels, however, have a better grasp of the divine plan than the human person who is limited by the sluggish nature of human intelligence; for they see the plan of providence in its principle, that is, in the vision of the divine nature. And so God employs angels to move man according to the plan of providence, a plan of which they too are a part, but which they grasp in a way that the human person cannot. Angels do not, however, move man's will; only God can move the will. For if my will could be moved by some limited creature outside me, it would not be my act of the will. But angels can move the imagination, they can inspire, protect, enlighten, and console.

Angels are not limited by space and time as man is; they are not subject to the limits of material existence, and so they can be servants of providence in ways that are not open to man by virtue of his limitations, just as man can be an instrument of providence in a way that is not open to a brute animal. Angels do not reason from premises to conclusions, as is characteristic of human intelligence. Rather, angels intuit; for they are created with the perfection of their knowledge from the beginning. They are present to material things by their attention, not by proximity within space, and they are not limited by time since time is the measure of physical motion, and angels are not physical. They are not temporal, but rather eviternal, a duration midway between time and eternity. Finally, they are inconceivably more intelligent than the most brilliant human being and more powerful than a human army.

All of recorded history is nothing but a collection of thin fibers that provide a very limited peek at aspects of God's providential plan. When we consider that each individual has only a very limited, foggy, broken apprehension of history, we begin to realize that it is simply not in man's ability to grasp the plan of providence. A leader of a nation, moreover, has only a very limited grasp of what is actually going on in the country that he governs, not to mention a very limited grasp of what is happening in the world at large: "It is hard enough for us to work out what is on earth, laborious to know what lies within our reach; who, then, can discover what is in the heavens?" (Ws 9, 16). But the superior intelligence of an angel could conceivably be specified to apprehend much more about particular human beings or the behaviour of nations throughout a number of centuries than man is able to apprehend.

The King, Knights, Bishops and Pawns

What does all this mean in the end? For one, it means that "all things work for good for those who love God" (Rm 8, 28). In other words, evil cannot have the final word over the lives of those who choose to surrender to divine providence.

How do we know this? Consider the following analogy. If I were to play a game of chess with a world-class chess champion and I knew every move that he was going to make in response to my own moves, and if I could apprehend the entire game at a glance, it would be impossible for me to lose the game. In fact, let's take this a step further. Not only do I know what moves my opponent is going to make, I also move his arm so that he can move his pieces. Again, there is no way that I could lose the game. It is in my power to orchestrate the entire game in such a way that victory is mine; for I know his moves and I am the cause of his moving those very pieces to the squares to which he freely chooses to move them.

Now this analogy falls short in that there is no conceivable way for me to move the arm of my opponent without determining his move. But God moves the will of man without determining him; man determines himself by choosing freely. But nothing has being, including man's free choices, without God acting as First Cause of its being. Thus, God knows eternally, in the eternal present, what free moves we "will" make. And so God cannot lose the game which He orchestrates. Should a person freely but maliciously choose to bang loudly on a drum, or clash symbols, while others choose to play a sweet and haunting melody, God merely arranges their order around the melody so that the drum beats and clashing, by virtue of their place within the whole, contribute to the beauty of the symphony.

Man is a pawn in a much larger game—a free pawn, but a pawn nonetheless—, and he has almost no idea what is happening on that level. As de Caussade writes: "The history of the world is nothing but the history of the war waged by the powers of the world and of hell since the beginning against the souls humbly devoted to the divine action. In this war, the advantages seem all on the side of pride, and yet humility always wins the day."₄₂ It is for us to surrender to divine providence, to cooperate with divine grace and do our small but significant part within that order. Like well disposed matter that is more useful to the builder, a man who is well disposed by the virtues, who is obedient and humble, self-controlled, patient and just, etc., is a much better instrument in the hands of providence. As de Caussade writes: "Since we know that the divine action embraces everything, directs everything, indeed does everything, apart from sin, faith has the duty of adoring, loving and welcoming it in everything."₄₃ The principal task of the spiritual life is to become more perfectly disposed, to learn to surrender ourselves more completely to the Spirit of God.

This game that God plays cannot be lost. The orchestration that He conducts cannot but deliver the most beautiful piece that will glorify Him in a way that, again, currently exceeds our imagination. Our joy will be that we were a part of that symphony, a part of the winning side of a highly complex chess game. By the end of the game, most of the pieces will have been sacrificed—as is typical in chess—, but only for the sake of final victory. Consider the death of any one of God's holy ones and note the fruits of such a sacrifice: "Precious in the eyes of the Lord is the death of his faithful ones" (Ps 116, 15). But all those who freely choose to walk in darkness place themselves outside the order of salvation and into the order of justice. They are destined to lose, and it is this loss that will be their inheritance for all eternity.

Chapter 12: A Note on Purgatory

A priest of a nearby diocese was once accosted by a woman who had purchased a Mass for her deceased father. What upset her was that during the Mass, the priest implied that her father was in purgatory: "What right do you have to say that my father is in purgatory?" she asked. He replied, "You are the one that told me he was in purgatory". She looked puzzled. "When did I say that?" she asked. He said, "You requested a Mass for him; if your father is in heaven, he doesn't need a Mass; and if he's in hell, all the Masses in the world won't do him any good. So if you requested that a Mass be said for the repose of his soul, it can only mean that you believe his soul is in purgatory."

Purgatory is an official doctrine of the Church. The Catechism describes it as the final purification of the elect, which is undergone "so as to achieve the holiness necessary to enter the joy of heaven" (sec. 1030). C.S. Lewis, who was not a Catholic, argued that our souls demand purgatory: "Would it not break the heart if God said to us, 'It is true, my son, that your breath smells and your rags drip with mud and slime, but we are charitable here and no one will upbraid you with these things, nor draw away from you. Enter into the joy'? Should we not reply, 'With submission, Sir, and if there is no objection, I'd rather be cleaned first.' 'It may hurt, you know.'- 'Even so, sir.'"[44]

Recently I was told of a great victory for the Church. It's the story of a man who about forty years ago decided to abandon the Church and all it represented, for the sake of his freedom. He'd decided that no one was going to tell him what to do, how to choose, what is right and wrong, etc., and he chose to raise his children on the same attitude.

About thirty five years later, though, he found himself pointing a loaded gun to his head. His life had become so empty and intolerable that he was simply going to end it. He does not know why, but he did not end his life that day. Instead, he sought professional help.

It was his psychiatrist, however, who finally made the suggestion that he think back to the choices that he'd made years ago that brought him to the point of suicide, and then choose the reverse, do the opposite, and see what happens. He thought about it for a while and realized that this would mean returning to the Church, to the sacraments, and allowing the Church to tell him what is morally right and wrong, etc. And so he went to a Church one night and listened.

This man now speaks of a profound joy in his life, a joy that increases with every passing day. But he also tells of the sorrow he feels deep within, a sorrow that also seems to increase with each passing day as he is forced to take note of the ruined lives of his children, raised as they were within the secular and permissive household of a practical atheist.

It is this combination of joy and sorrow that can help explain the simultaneous suffering and joy that is experienced by the souls in purgatory. St. Catherine of Genoa says that the pain of purgatory is greater than any pain that can be experienced on earth. But she also says that the pain of purgatory is more joyful than the greatest joys on earth. The joy of purgatory comes from knowing that eternal life is ours, that we will enjoy a happiness that exceeds our capacity to imagine and which will never end. The sorrow of purgatory comes from—among other things—knowing fully the harm that our sins have caused others as well as the complete awareness of the stains left on our soul, which render us unfit and unable to tolerate being in the presence of pure Innocence Itself.

Allow me to imagine that I am a window. During the night I see nothing wrong with myself; anyone can look through me and see the outside world. But as the sun begins to rise and its rays begin to penetrate me, I see all sorts of stains, finger prints, dried spittle, dirt, etc., that I didn't notice before. All I can do is hope that someone will come along and wipe me clean, because if someone were to look out the window at this point, their vision would be obscured, distorted, and they would find me rather cumbersome; for my stains prevent the beauty of the world outside of me, which I am bound to channel, from being fully appreciated.

My stains would torment me, but I would be helpless to do anything about them. Try to magnify that pain a thousandfold, and we might achieve a glimpse of the pain that is in store for us in purgatory, if we're one of the lucky ones to make it there. And perhaps the only way the window can be cleaned is through the heat of the sun itself; it must shine so brightly and get so hot that the stains and dirt are completely burned away. It is because the dirty window is so unlike the sun that it experiences its heat and brilliance as painful.

Consider, too, the pain of wanting to right certain wrongs that we recognize we were responsible for, but are unable to right immediately. A person with a just will refuses to accept rest until those wrongs and the damage they have caused are made right, which is why the souls in purgatory accept their suffering—caused by the knowledge of those wrongs—until all of them are made right, which in most cases would take decades, some even centuries. The essence of purgatory's sorrow is summed up by poet John Greenleaf Whittier (1807-92): "For of all sad words of tongue or pen, the saddest are these: 'It might have been!'"

One pain that is likely in store for most of us is the frustration that will come from the awareness that the living have the ability to grant us tremendous relief by offering fasts, alms, prayers, i.e., The Rosary, The Act of Reparation, The Acts of Faith, Hope, and Charity, The

Stations of the Cross, and The Sacrifice of the Mass, etc., in suffrage for us, but are not doing so because they don't realize they have this power to help us, nor that there is a spiritual treasury of the Church available for them to relieve us, nor that we even need their help, because we did not pass on to them these enduring truths of the faith.

Praying for the dead is a devout and holy thought (2 M 12: 45), and offering the sacrifice of the Mass for a departed soul is "an action all together fine and noble" (2 M 12: 43). Moreover, it is one of the spiritual works of mercy. Unless our deceased parents, relatives, and friends were people of extraordinary virtue and holiness, it is probably a good idea to remember to offer them works of suffrage for about the next forty years or so. Their gratitude will be unending.

Chapter 13: A Few Thoughts on the Existence and Nature of Hell

My friend, the late Monsignor Tom Wells of the Archdiocese of Washington, would often read parts of James Joyce's *A Portrait of the Artist as a Young Man* to his students. In it we find a sermon describing the pains of hell that rivals St. John Bosco's dream on the same subject. Some students had actually remarked to my friend that hearing Father Arnall's sermon read to them was probably the most significant thing that had ever happened to them in all their years of Catholic education.

So I thought it would be a good idea to read it myself. After doing so, I decided never to read it to students. I changed my mind eventually and read it out loud on one occasion—after my students pleaded for me to read it to them—I might have had a drug dealer or two in the classroom at the time, and since one cannot reason with a drug dealer, why not try to scare them out of their wits and possibly back to their senses? The read is rather disturbing, so disturbing in fact that one tends to wonder about the divine love. But how is it possible to accurately describe the suffering of the damned without losing sight of God's boundless mercy?

There are many signs of the divine love for human persons, but few are wont to consider Hell one of them. Consider, though, that hell is in fact one of the greatest signs of God's love for us. If God is Love (1 Jn 4, 8), then it is impossible for hell **not** to exist; for love isn't love unless it is freely given. If God willed us into existence for the sake of an eternal union with Himself grounded in love, then it follows that we have the ability to reject and miss that destiny.

Imagine the very real possibility of falling in love with someone who, you eventually discover, simply couldn't care less about you, or whether you disappeared off the face of the earth. If you truly love that person, you will not force him to love you. It is not possible to be satisfied with a person who is forced to love you; for such a relationship is meaningless, because love isn't love unless it is freely given. Love demands that you allow the one who refuses your love to have his will. It is no different with God. He loves us so much that He will allow us to reject Him for all eternity.

And so Christ's teaching on hell is consistent with reason. But what are we to make of the scriptural images of hell, "...where there will be weeping and grinding of teeth" (Mt 8, 12), "...where their worm never dies, and the fire is never quenched" (Mk 9, 48), "...the lake that burns with fire and sulfur, which is the second death" (Rv 21, 8)? What do these images really signify?

Character and Destiny

The first point to keep in mind is the soul's indestructibility. To make a long story short, the soul has a faculty or power (the mind) that acts independently of matter, and that activity is thinking. If the mind can act independently of matter, it can exist independently of matter, since activity follows upon being. Hence, the soul endures when the body is destroyed.

Now man's destiny is to know and love the highest being (God), and his happiness consists precisely in this knowledge and love and in the journey towards it. To possess God in the Beatific Vision is to have no need of anything else.

But the human person has to freely choose to love God. He cannot freely do so if He sees God directly; for the will would necessarily cling to God were it to behold the Supreme Good as He is in Himself. That is why the human person is required to choose his destiny, "to work out his salvation", within the order of time. It is only within this order that he can freely determine himself towards God, or reject God by making himself the center of his existence.

To direct one's life towards union with God, the human person must commit to complete loyalty to human goods, not just his own good. Willing only the realization of my own good does not constitute a good will. I am a good person by virtue of my willing the entire spectrum of human goods, and that spectrum is not limited to this individual instance which is me. Nor is it limited to my immediate family, or relatives, or all those whom I know. If I will "the good", I do so wherever there is an instance of it, that is, I will the good of all human persons. That is why, for example, killing innocent non-combatants in order to bring a quick end to a war, or counseling an abortion in order to minimize the stress of a difficult situation, or euthanizing a handicapped child or a severely depressed adult in order to make one's own life easier or relieve suffering, are incompatible with loyalty to the good; for one may not do evil that good may come of it. So too, cowardliness, over-indulgence, allowing idleness to destroy noble aspirations, selfishness, partiality and hostility are incompatible with a will loyal to the good. In such cases, our loyalty is deficient, fragmented, and arbitrary. The hearts of the wicked are focused more on the self that is an individual instance of a human good, than on "human good" as such.

There is no other way to the fulfillment of our destiny than through character, and there is nothing we should value more than its quality. In fact, if people were to value their character as much as they value their lawns, gardens, or automobiles, we'd be living in heaven on earth.

But character is not the same as personality. It is very possible for a person to have a great personality, but bad character; it is also possible for a person of good character to have a miserable personality. Character is entirely determined by oneself, that is, by one's freely chosen moral actions. There is nothing that belongs more intimately to us, nothing that is more "our own" than our moral identity, or character. Environmental factors and inherited traits are not chosen, and indeed they determine much that is within us; but our character is determined by how we have chosen to relate to all these factors that determine us. I have known plenty of people who have been brought up terribly, who came from horribly broken environments, and who are terribly wounded, as is to be expected. But many of them have endured all this with their good character intact. Conversely, there are many who have come from very loving and safe environments, but who have made commitments that are hateful, immoral, and unjust.

Now, we tend to enjoy being in the presence of those who are like us in character. In fact, friendships are founded upon common qualities and interests, especially a common moral identity. When a relationship is attempted and fails, the reason is often that the two "did not have much in common". What does all this mean? It means that it is possible to determine for oneself a character so deficient that one finds it painful to be in the presence of those with morally beautiful or noble character. Thus, one would find it painful to be in the presence of the communion of saints. As an analogy from the realm of musical taste, imagine a punk rocker sitting through an opera, or Stravinsky at a Marilyn Manson concert. Both would likely be very uncomfortable. Or, consider a person who freely and deliberately fostered racist sentiments throughout his entire life, against Jews, or black people. When he dies, he discovers that everyone in heaven is Jewish, or black. Could such a person be comfortable in this heaven? Clearly not. Thus, in some ways hell is but another instance of the mercy of God.

The failure to be open to the entire spectrum of human goods (human life, truth, leisure, sociability, religion, marriage, and integrity) as a result of free choices that are unjust, or hostile, or lazy, or intemperate, or vengeful, or irreverent, or self-centered, or envious, or avaricious, or squeamish, self-deceiving, vindictive, resentful, or impatient, is to freely harm our relationship to God who is the Supreme Good, to render it either non-existent, seriously wounded, or weakened.

The Pain of Hell

The pain of hell is rooted in the fact that our nature naturally seeks rest but does not find it, because the will has cut itself off from its only source of rest. The Beatific Vision is precisely that rest. The damned have freely deprived themselves of that beatitude by virtue of choices that have ill disposed them to communion with the saints, choices that can be translated as a rejection of friendship with God. It is as if a plant, that had the capacity to know itself and feed itself, refused to water itself, thus ill disposing itself to further life.

The damned have an inordinate love of themselves, for they loved themselves for their own sake, but chose not to love others for their own sake, but subordinated them to their own ends, to be used in one way or another. At the same time the damned cannot help but loath themselves. In so far as evil is a deficiency, a privation, a kind of non-being, it follows that as a person plunges more deeply into sin and darkness, the more depraved he becomes. But the more depraved a person becomes, the less there is in himself to love. Thus, the pain of hell includes the pain of self-loathing. One does not like what one has created.

To get a glimpse of what the pain hell might be like, let us try to do the impossible. It is impossible to

167

imagine eternity or eviternity; for eternity is the present alone, without past or future, and not time without end, as we usually conceive of it. But eternity is forever, the forever "now", and the only "forever" that is somewhat imaginable—but not entirely—is "time without end". So consider having to endure forever a slight discomfort, such as a cold or a feeling of boredom. Begin by imagining what it would be like to endure it for a year, then two, then ten, then one hundred, then one thousand, then ten thousand. Ten thousand years already exceeds the capacity of the human imagination. Finally, consider having to endure this slight discomfort forever, without end. That means that after a billion years, or ten billion, hell hasn't even begun. It simply does not end.

The pain of self-hatred and restlessness is much worse than the pain of a bad cold or feeling of boredom. To have to endure that self-imposed suffering forever, without any hope of an end, could accurately be compared to a gnawing worm that never dies, or to a fire that is never quenched.

Father Arnall employs a rather effective metaphor.

You have often seen the sand on the seashore. How fine are its tiny grains! And how many of those tiny little grains go to make up the small handful which a child grasps, in its play. Now imagine a mountain of that sand, ... imagine such an enormous mass of countless particles of sand multiplied as often as there are leaves in the forest, ... and imagine that at the end of every million years a little bird came to that mountain and carried away in its beak a tiny grain of that sand. How many millions upon millions of centuries would pass before that bird had carried away even a square foot of that mountain, how many eons upon eons of ages before it had carried away all. Yet at the end of that immense stretch of time not even one instant of eternity could be said to have ended.[45]

The pain of hell also includes the suffering of having to endure bad company as well as the pain of loneliness. There is not an ounce of benevolence in hell. God is Love, but the damned have deliberately and persistently refused God's offer of Himself. And so they cannot love anything that belongs to God. Thus, they hate one another. Father Arnall continues:

> Consider finally, that the torment of this infernal prison is increased by the company of the damned themselves. Evil company on earth is so noxious that even the plants, as if by instinct, withdraw from the company of whatsoever is deadly or hurtful to them. In hell all laws are overturned: there is no thought of family or country, of ties, of relationships. ... their ... rage intensified by the presence of beings ... raging like themselves. All sense of humanity is forgotten. ... The mouths of the damned are full of blasphemies against God and of hatred for their fellow sufferers and of curses against those souls which were their accomplices in sin.[46]

The more we consider the pain of loss enduring forever, the greater the chance of catching a glimpse of the horror of hell. But to appreciate the justice of hell requires an understanding of the rottenness of sin. Indeed, sin is rotten, but very few of us if any fully appreciate its seriousness. We are little more than dust and ashes, completely and utterly dependent upon God for continued existence, and everything we have and are is pure gift. On top of the sheer gift of human existence, we have been re-created (redeemed) for a supernatural happiness that is so great that we cannot begin to conceive of it here. To make that happiness possible again—after the fall of man—, the Second Person of the Trinity joined a human nature in order to undergo a horrible death. Life Itself destroyed death by entering into it, tasting it, and conquering it by rising, and yet we still manage to convince ourselves that we can do things our way instead of God's way, that we can still live every day of our lives without centering it around a commitment of perpetual thanksgiving to God, without making every effort to live in accordance with divine law. That depravity spreads like cancer undetected so that after a time the truths of the gospel begin to make us very uncomfortable. And this is the evidence that we have taken a wrong turn somewhere along the way.

But hell cannot be unjust, because it is the loss of pure gift, and no one has a right to a gift. Moreover, it is a loss that was brought about as a result of our own free and mysterious will. It is forever because eternity or eviternity has no future, and so the will that enters it opposed to the will of God is forever fixed as such.

It is impossible to judge the status of an individual person's relationship to God; in fact, we are never entirely certain of the status of our own. One reason is that our capacity for self-deception is remarkably acute. There always seems to be an unbecoming mixture of the sacred and the profane in the lives of ordinary believers. The true believer struggles against these vices and mistakes when made aware of them and is committed to purifying his life of them. But some are not committed to this at all, but are relatively indifferent to it and have given themselves to flirting with secularism and a relatively mild form of hedonism. Some, even believers, have decided not to allow certain aspects of their lives to be scrutinized or challenged in any way. They might be entirely open to reforming social structures and raising taxes, for example, but have a priest dare to challenge their sex lives from the pulpit and watch how many nasty and unsigned letters he and his bishop receive the following week. And then there are those who have given themselves over to evil. These latter can be simultaneously committed to all sorts of goods and good causes (for there is no such thing as total evil). A successful abortionist, for example, can be committed to his family, and be an active member of the community, and coach little league baseball. He might very well have convinced himself that his work is necessary and contributes to the common good. But this should not be confused with a judgment of conscience; for it is little more than a shining example of our capacity for self-deception.

The Good News about Sin

A former ethics professor once told me that it takes a great deal of character to be able to admit that one was wrong. This becomes much harder to do the older we get. It is one thing to look back a year or two and admit that one was mistaken, but it is a very different matter to have to look back at the last twenty five or so years and face the fact that one was wrong about something for that length of time. Humility is a childlike quality. Perhaps that is why this virtue becomes more difficult as we move away from childhood into adulthood. It is not often that we come across an adult with such strength of character as to be so at ease with his own finitude and so open to truth that the opportunity for growth has more appeal than the security of not having to gaze upon his own imperfection.

But there is a kind of good news about sin. Our route to great character can be very short, and our own sins, imperfections, and errors can be the vehicle to this new and higher stature. St. Therese of Lisieux, whom Pope Pius X regarded as "the greatest saint in modern times" and who is now a Doctor of the Church, was fully aware of this. She writes: "I am no longer surprised at anything, nor do I grieve at seeing that I am frailty itself; on the contrary I glory in it, and expect to discover new imperfections in myself each day. These lights concerning my nothingness do me more good, I affirm, than lights regarding faith".[47]

The greatest and most influential human beings in history were precisely those who took this short route to greatness by daring to gaze upon their own sinfulness, imperfections, and errors and acknowledge them, such as St. Paul, St. Justin Martyr, St. Jerome, St. Ambrose, St. Augustine, or more recently Ronald Knox, G.K. Chesterton, and Jacques Maritain, easily three of the greatest thinkers of the twentieth century. One of the most moving examples of rising from darkness to moral heroism is Dr. Bernard N. Nathanson. He says of himself: "I am personally responsible for 75,000 abortions. ... I was one of the founders of the National Association for the Repeal of the Abortion Laws in the U.S. in 1968. A truthful poll of opinion then would have found that most Americans were against permissive abortion. Yet within five years we had convinced the Supreme Court to issue the decision which legalized abortion throughout America in 1973 and produced virtual abortion on demand up to birth."[48]

He openly tells of his involvement in the deliberate and systematic creation of lies designed to deceive the American public and eventually the Supreme Court of the United States, and he confesses that his tactics included persuading the media that the cause of permissive abortion was liberal, enlightened, and sophisticated. He fabricated the results of fictional polls on the number of illegal abortions done annually in the U.S., and on the number of women dying from them. He speaks of how he was involved in the systematic vilification of the Catholic Church and its "socially backward ideas" and his participation in the denigration and suppression of all scientific evidence that life begins at conception.

But Nathanson became the world's most powerful and influential defender of life and advocate for the unborn. This same man who ran the largest abortion clinic in the Western world would later write:

> It is clear that permissive abortion is purposeful destruction of what is undeniably human life. It is an impermissible act of deadly violence. One must concede that unplanned pregnancy is a wrenchingly difficult dilemma. But to look for its solution in a deliberate act of destruction is to trash the vast resourcefulness of human ingenuity, and to surrender the public weal to the classic utilitarian answer to social problems. As a scientist I know, not believe, know that human life begins at conception. Although I am not a formal religionist, I believe with all my heart that there is a divinity of existence which commands us to declare a final and irreversible halt to this infinitely sad and shameful crime against humanity.[49]

Nathanson's heroism has nothing to do with his fame, but everything to do with his humility. Had he remained entirely unknown, his character would not be any the less for it. The difficulty that accompanies the decision to humbly open oneself up to the reform of one's character is richly rewarded with insight, a much deeper integrity, and a far more influential and fruitful existence.

Finally, I think it can be argued that as a culture, we tend not to take free-choice and personal responsibility too seriously. This is especially evident in the way we treat, judicially, violent crime; we continue to attribute the causes of criminal behavior to environmental factors outside the criminal himself, rather than to the will— indeed, doing so is far less frightening. Consider the number of "rages" we've fabricated over the years: road rage, air rage, rink rage, office rage, desk rage, work rage, bike rage, abandonment rage, rejection rage, etc. "Something just came over me," is typically the line of defense employed by offenders, and many continue to fall for it. The label makes it much easier to hide the fact that such aggression was rooted ultimately in nothing other than good ole fashioned free-choice.

But God does take free-choice seriously, because He is a lover who gives us His undivided attention at every instant of our lives and offers us sufficient grace to enter into His friendship. It is really only up to us to take it or leave it, and He loves us enough to allow us our decision: "I call heaven and earth to witness against you today that I have set before you life and death, blessings and curses. Choose life so that you and your descendants may live, loving the Lord your God, obeying him, and holding fast to him" (Dt 29, 19-20).

Chapter 14: On the Happiness of Heaven

The happiness of heaven exceeds our ability to imagine and articulate. For St. Paul says: "What eye has not seen, and ear has not heard, and what has not entered the human heart, what God has prepared for those who love him" (1 Co 2, 9). But just as we can come to some understanding of God indirectly, that is, by considering what He is not, so too can we come to a very real understanding of the happiness of heaven by a similar negative method, that is, by coming to understand what happiness is and what the happiness of heaven is not. Allow me to begin with a few points on human happiness.

A person is an individual substance of a rational nature (Boethius). A man is a person. He has the capacity to know and to love. Knowledge and love are two ways that the human person expands or becomes larger, and happiness has everything to do with personal expansion or enlargement.

To know something outside of you, such as the oak tree in your front yard, is to be united to it in a certain way. Knowledge is in you, and so the thing you know (oak tree) is in you, but not in the same way it exists outside of you—i.e., the oak tree does not exist in you physically, but mentally (as a concept). The tree, or whatever it is we are knowing, exists in the mind immaterially, which is why Aristotle said that the mind becomes in a way all things.

In other words, in knowledge, you and I become something other than ourselves without ceasing to be ourselves. And so knowledge is a kind of expansion or enlargement of the self. And as Aristotle says in his first line of his Metaphysics, "All men by nature desire to know". In other words, all men by nature desire to become more than they are.

The difference between knowing and eating is that eating results in the destruction of its object, while knowledge does not. Moreover, eating results in the physical enlargement of the self, while knowledge brings about a spiritual or mental expansion.

The reason all men by nature desire to know is that "good" is a property of being. Just as rationality is a property of man, and growth is a property of living things, so too is "good" a property of being, so that whatever exists is good, in so far as it exists. The good is an object of desire, and all things desire, at a basic level, to be most fully, which is why plants strive to keep themselves alive via nutrition and why animals hunt for food and run from danger, etc. And that is why man desires to know, because knowledge is a way to exist more fully, that is, to be more than what one currently is, without ceasing to be what one is. It is a way to be more perfectly.

It follows from the above that man naturally loves himself; for to love another is to will the good of another. We naturally will the best for ourselves, that is, we naturally will our own perfection. Now, we know ourselves as persons with the capacity for knowing, and so we know ourselves as incomplete and thus open to expansion. We also know others as beings of the same nature as ourselves, that is, as human persons. But we don't necessarily love them as we love ourselves. To love them as another self is to will the best for them as we will the best for ourselves. And just as we will the best for ourselves for our own sake, to love another as another self is to will his good for his sake, not for the sake of what that might do for me. But to love the other as another self is something that one can only decide to do or not to do; it is not something that occurs necessarily, but by choice.

To decide to love the other as another self, however, is to become that person without ceasing to be myself.

In knowledge, the other exists in me as known, but in love, I exist outside myself as him. His good (his well-being) has become my good, and so if I love him, I will his well-being and rejoice in it.

This too is a kind of self-expansion, an enlargement of the self. If I refuse to love the other for his sake, but choose, rather, to love myself for my sake and the other only for what he or she does for me, then I do not love the other as another self. And so I have not become the other; I have not expanded. My love for the other is much like my love for food, which I love for my sake, not for the good of the food; for we do not destroy what we love, but we destroy food in the process of eating it. The love we have for food and drink is nothing more than self-love.

And so true disinterested love is the love of the other for his sake, not for my sake, and it is this love that achieves a real enlargement of the self. Now to exist is good, but to exist more fully is better. And so a rational kind of existence is better than a non-rational kind of existence; it is better to be a person than to be a plant. And since happiness is another word for "well-being", happiness has to do with being most fully. To be happy is to exist well.

Now, to know is good, but to know and love is even better. It follows that the greater our knowledge and love, the larger we are, and thus the happier we are.

There is something more noble about love of another than knowledge considered by itself. As was said above, when something is known, it exists in me in a new way; but when I love another person as another self, I exist outside myself as him, without ceasing to be myself. And so love involves a kind of ecstasy. The very word ecstasy comes from the Greek, *ekstasis*, which means "to be outside oneself". In order to love someone as another self, I have to first know him as someone like myself, and so the self-expansion involved in the love of another can only occur in addition to the self-expansion involved in knowing. Hence, love achieves a greater self-expansion than does knowledge alone. That is why we all agree that a knowledgeable person is not necessarily a good or noble person.

And so the more we love others for their sake (disinterestedly), the larger we become and thus the better we become, and the happier we become. The more we "exit" ourselves in a genuinely disinterested love of the other, the more ecstatic life becomes.

Notice how this rings true to our own experience. If I truly love another, such as my daughter, as another me, then her happiness becomes my own, and so I genuinely delight in her well-being. When she is happy, I am happy. Consider someone you truly love and recall how happy you are to discover that this person has become truly happy. The more people we love with this kind of selfless love, it only follows that the happier we will become, for our happiness will be doubled, and tripled, and quadrupled, etc.

There are a variety of ways to become more than what one currently is. This is another way of saying that there are certain intrinsic goods that perfect us as human persons. One's own physical life can become better, or healthier. The possession of truth, as we said above, involves an expansion of the self, whether that turns out to be scientific, historical, philosophical, or theological truth, etc. One is raised up or taken outside of oneself (*ekstasis*) through the contemplation of the beautiful, as we might find in beautiful music, poetry, scenery, photography, or paintings, etc. The production of works and the development of our natural talents for certain activities (mechanical, musical, athletic, etc.) perfects us as human persons.

Of course we become more than what we are considered individually through relationships grounded in love, such as friendships, acquaintances, and in our relationship to our parents and particularly to the civil community as a whole. In fact, an element of our own happiness is the feeling of having a debt that cannot be paid. Without that feeling, one lacks gratitude, and without gratitude, our relationship to our parents and to the civil community as a whole is not what is can and ought to be.

In marriage, two become one flesh, one body, something much more than an individual considered in himself. Moral integrity, which is the harmony that exists between reason and one's choices, is a higher good than any of the previously mentioned, and it is fundamentally related to the highest intrinsic human good, which is the virtue of religion, which is the virtue by which one renders due worship and reverence to God, the source of all that is good and who is Goodness Itself.

Those who choose to love the good itself, not merely their "delectable" good, will be moved to seek the giver behind the gifts that enrich their lives and of which they know they are not the cause. And so on a natural level they seek the face of God: "Who shall climb the mountain of the Lord? Who shall stand in his holy place? The man with clean hands and pure heart, who desires not worthless things, who has not sworn so as to deceive his neighbor. He shall receive blessings from the Lord and reward from the God who saves him. Such are the men who seek him, seek the face of the God of Jacob" (Ps 24, 3-6).[50]

To seek to know God, to seek His approval (favor), is to seek His face. But we cannot find it directly on our own. Nevertheless, something of His face is discerned in his effects, just as we form an image of a person's face, whom we've never met, in the reading of his correspondence, or in his works: "For what can be known about God is evident to them, because God made it evident to them. Ever since the creation of the world, his invisible attributes of eternal power and divinity have been able to be understood and perceived in what he has made" (Rm 1, 19-20). Moreover, as St. Bernard writes: "Reason and natural justice alike move me to give up myself wholly to loving Him to whom I owe all that I have and am. But faith shows me that I should love Him far more than I love myself, as I come to realize that He hath given me not my own life only, but even Himself. Yet, before the time of full revelation had come, before the Word was made flesh, died on the Cross, came forth from the grave, and returned to His Father; before God had shown us how much He loved us by all this plenitude of grace, the commandment had been uttered, 'Thou shalt love the Lord thy God with all thine heart, and with all thy soul and with all thy might' (Deut. 6:5), that is, with all thy being, all thy knowledge, all thy powers. And it was not unjust for God to claim this from His own work and gifts. Why should not the creature love his Creator, who gave him the power to love? Why should he not love Him with all his being, since it is by His gift alone that he can do anything that is good?"[51]

Forever Satiated and Forever Thirsty

Although we might seek the face of God as the cause of all the goods of the physical universe, knowing God intuitively or directly, as He is in Himself, exceeds the capacity of human nature. This means that we depend on God to freely and gratuitously grant us a sharing in His divine nature (grace), which is supernatural. But this dependency on the gratuity of another—in this case God's gratuitous self-giving—is something that we already know through our natural friendships, as well as through our parents and the social whole. Our natural happiness, which is an imperfect happiness, is dependent upon the gratuitous self-giving of others, for we cannot force anyone to receive our love, that is, to be our friends; love isn't love unless it is freely given. And we know the feeling of having a debt that cannot be paid in full, both with respect to our parents as well as to the civil community as a whole, in particular with regard to the sacrifices of countless others (i.e., soldiers) who have gone before us, etc., and that feeling, which when welcomed translates into gratitude, is also an element of our happiness.

How much more is this gratuitous element and the feeling of having a debt that cannot be fully repaid an essential part of the supernatural happiness that comes from knowing and loving God directly in the Beatific Vision? And so man's complete and utter fulfillment consists in the possession of God through direct knowledge and love, and this depends upon the divine initiative to lift him beyond the powers of his limited nature through divine grace and reveal Himself to him in the Beatific Vision. St. Alphonsus Liguori writes: "The glory of heaven consists in seeing and loving God face to face....The reward which God promises to us, does not consist altogether in the beauty, the harmony, and other advantages of the city of Paradise. God himself, whom the saints are allowed to behold, is, according to the promise made to Abraham, the principal reward of the just in heaven."[52]

God is the source of all that is good, and since the effect cannot exceed the cause, He contains within Himself all the perfections of the created order; these perfections exist in God as God. For example, beauty exists in God not as a property, but as God. And so God is Beauty Itself. And since God is without limits, God is Beauty without limit. It follows that there is no beauty that can exist which exceeds the beauty of God.

So too is God Goodness Itself, as well as Truth Itself. To know Truth Itself and to possess Goodness Itself and to contemplate Beauty Itself is to achieve a perfect and unimaginable happiness. It is simply not possible to desire other finite goods for our own fulfillment, goods that are not God, when we possess the Supreme, Perfect, and Unlimited Good.[53]

The goods we sacrifice here, in this life, for the sake of eternal life will be possessed by the blessed in eternal life, but these goods will possess an inconceivably richer mode of existence, for we will possess them in God, who is Goodness Itself, because He is Being Itself. For example, the religious who vows chastity and poverty will possess all the goods he or she sacrifices in a much higher way in God. For example, the good of sexual union, which is a marital act, is an echo of a much higher good; for there is much more to sexual union than the temporary pleasure of orgasm. It is a union of persons, and it achieves a profound and exclusive intimacy; in short, it is a kind of knowledge—we speak of carnal knowledge. Sexual union in marital intimacy is a kind of connatural knowledge (an interior knowledge of the other that is always more than what can be articulated in words). The point, however, is that all that the marital act imparts to married couples—an intimate and blessed knowledge of the other as well as the joy of being intimately known, a knowledge that is too deep for words—is possessed in heaven in a superabundance that exceeds the capacity of the sexual act to impart. Similarly, poverty for the sake of the kingdom of God is rewarded exceedingly, because to possess God in eternity is to possess everything.

It is possible for us to get a tiny glimpse of this through prayer—at least a certain level and intensity of prayer.[54] Sometimes a person becomes so entranced by the goodness and beauty of God in prayer, a goodness and beauty that he or she has come to apprehend through a life of faith and the light that belongs to faith, that he or she desires nothing else but to rest in God for as long as possible. At such times, one does not wish to engage in any kind of activity except that of prayer, which at this level is a resting in God. It is at such times that one begins to understand that the happiness of heaven is a perfect resting in God (Cf. Heb 3, 11).

But this rest does not imply a cessation of desire. Rather, it involves a cessation of *a certain kind of desire*, that is, desire that is part and parcel of the state of imperfection, that is, the state of being on the way to God. In heaven, one does not desire the perfect good as if one does not possess it, but one desires God in a way that is consistent with the possession of God. St. Alphonsus Liguori writes:

> But the joys of Paradise constantly satiate and content the heart. "I shall be satisfied when thy glory shall appear" (Ps 16, 15). And though they satiate, they always appear to be as new as the first time they were experienced: they are always enjoyed and always desired, always desired and always possessed. "Satiety", says St. Gregory, "accompanies desire" (Mor., bk 18, ch. 18). Thus, the desires of the saints in Paradise do not beget pain, because they are always satisfied; and satiety does not produce disgust, because it is always accompanied with desire. Hence the soul shall be always satiated and always thirsty: she shall be for ever thirsty and always satiated with delights.[55]

St. Bernard also writes: "Here indeed is appeasement without weariness: here never-quenched thirst for knowledge, without distress; here eternal and infinite desire which knows no want; here, finally, is that sober inebriation which comes not from drinking new wine but from enjoying God".[56]

But all this does not really capture the happiness of heaven from the inside, so to speak. Yet I believe we can do so, to some extent at least, by analogy, and the best place to begin is by considering the happiness or ecstasy that results from a genuinely disinterested love.

To love another disinterestedly, as we said above, is to will his good, at least as much as I will my own. To will his good is to will that he be most fully (to be fully good, and fully beautiful). Obviously this includes the will that the other know his goodness and delight in it, that is, to be happy. To know that the one we love is as happy as he deserves to be makes us happy, if we truly love him.

Now, to praise another is to acknowledge his goodness. Praising another expresses the delight we take in his goodness. If the other does not delight in his own goodness because he is not fully aware of it, we praise him in order to acknowledge what he has yet to acknowledge, because we want him—or her, of course—to delight or rejoice in that goodness. We praise our children because we want them to know their own goodness as we know it and to be as happy as they deserve to be. To praise another genuinely is to share in his happiness, or to help make him as happy as we'd like him to be—as happy as we are, if not more so.

There is a certain oneness in this—one knowledge (he and I both know his goodness), and one joy (he and I both rejoice in his goodness). In other words, I delight in his glory, and if his goodness is recognized by others, I delight in that acknowledgment, that he is being praised by others as he deserves. Moreover, I delight also that his happiness is increasing in this very acknowledgment and praise; for he is happy that he has pleased us, because he loves us too and does not want only to please himself. He is good, and so he wants that goodness to spread out beyond himself to others. He delights that we are delighted, and we are delighted that he is delighted and that his delight has been increased. We also may hope that it continues to increase, and knowing that it will only renders us increasingly happy.

That Our Principal Happiness in Heaven is in the Happiness of God

Charity is disinterested love of God; an intimate love of God under the aspect of personal friendship. Now friendship implies a certain common quality, and thus a certain equality. Divine grace is precisely this common quality that brings about a certain equality of sorts; for divine grace is a sharing in the divine nature. By divine grace we are raised to a supernatural level without ceasing to be human. In other words, grace renders us holy, and God is Holiness Itself.

Charity is the love of God for God's sake, not for our own. To love with charity is to love God because He is supremely good and deserving of love. Bishop Bossuet wrote: "It is agreed with the majority of the School that Charity is a love of God for himself, independently of the Beatitude to be found in him."[57]

St. Bernard of Clairvaux speaks of the four degrees of love, beginning with the love of self, moving on to the love of God for the sake of myself, to the love of God because God is good in Himself, and finally to the love of self in God. He writes: The third degree of love… is to love God on His own account, solely because He is God."[58] He continues: "The fourth degree of love is attained for ever when we love God only and supremely, when we do not even love ourselves except for God's sake; so that He Himself is the reward of them that love Him, the everlasting reward of an everlasting love."[59]

If we love God for His sake, we have "become Him" without ceasing to be ourselves; for all disinterested love is a "becoming the beloved" and thus a self-expansion. This "exit of self" towards "becoming Him" is only possible through His grace, for it is only through Him (His grace, which is a sharing in His divine nature) that we can "go out to meet Him" to love Him as another "self".[60]   God loves Himself in us. We do not will that He become most fully the Person He is meant to be, because He is that eternally, but we will His Supreme Goodness, we know It, affirm It, praise It, and delight in It, which He is perfectly and eternally. He is eternally and perfectly happy, and so we are happy that He is perfectly and eternally happy as He deserves and as no other creature deserves to be.

Hence, we share in His infinite happiness. That happiness is our greatest happiness.[61]   That He is joyful, that He is Joy Itself, renders us full of joy. The blessed see his glory, and they are happy that He is glorified in heaven and that all praise Him for His supreme goodness, for His mercy, His justice, His Love, His wisdom, His generosity, etc. That He is praised by so many only increases our joy.

And God is pleased by our praise, which adds nothing to His greatness, but He is pleased nonetheless, because He loves us, and our praise is good for us, although we praise Him not for our sake, but on account of Him. That He is pleased with us serves to increase our delight, because we love Him and want Him to be pleased, as a child is pleased that his father is pleased with him; for he loves his father and wants to please him. Hence, we are of one love, of one happiness, of one joy. This one joy is God's happiness, and it is God, since whatever is in God is identical to His act of existing. In short, His happiness is the cause of our joy; it is the principle of our happiness. That is why he says : " ...Come, enter into your master's joy' (Mt 25, 21)." We do not enter into our own joy, but a joy that is larger than ourselves, for God cannot be contained.

Now, not even the entire host of heaven can praise God as much as God deserves to be praised and loved. And that could become a source of sadness for us; our joy would be imperfect if this state of affairs went unrectified. But it is the Son who offers Him perfect praise that measures up to what He is deserving of. And so we delight in the Son's love of the Father. Our happiness is complete in the knowledge of the Son's perfect love of the Father, His perfect praise of Him. But such worship of the Son is also deserving of immeasurable praise and glory in return, and so we delight in the knowledge of the Father's love of the Son. It is a perfect love, a love and praise equal to what He deserves.

That praise of the Son has planted Itself on earthly soil (Calvary), and so now the earth offers the Father, in the Son, fitting and perfect praise. Creation may now achieve perfection in him who praises the Father perfectly and loves all things on account of Him, and for Him, that He may be perfectly loved and praised. And the Father loves all things on account of the Son, Jesus Christ, and for him, that he may be loved, praised, and glorified. And so all things were created through him and for him: "He is the image of the invisible God, the firstborn of all creation. For in him were created all things in heaven and on earth, the visible and the invisible, whether thrones or dominions or principalities or powers; all things were created through him and for him" (Col 1, 15-16).

The angels worship Him, and one angel's worship of Him is beautiful, but it does not do Him perfect justice, although He delights in it: "Lord, extolled in the heights by angelic powers, you are also praised by all earth's creatures, each in its own way. With all the splendor of heavenly worship, you still delight in such tokens of love as earth can offer. May heaven and earth together acclaim you as King. May the praise that is sung in heaven resound in the heart of every creature on earth" (from Liturgy of the Hours, Morning Prayer, Sunday, Week III).

187

The entire hierarchy of angels offers Him fitting praise because it is total, and that worship increases our joy, because our joy is in His happiness. But that praise and worship does not measure up to what He fully deserves; for He is deserving of infinite and omnipotent praise, the praise that only He, the Lord, can give. God the Son praises the Father, loves the Father, adores the Father, offers Himself to Him, and the Father loves the Son and glorifies Him as He deserves. This mutual love of the Father and the Son, the Holy Spirit, is our life in heaven. It is All for everyone and everyone's All (1 Co 15, 28).

On the Joy of Being Known

Aristotle understood that man's greatest happiness consists in the contemplation of the highest things. In his *Nicomachean Ethics*, he writes: "For while the whole life of the gods is blessed, and that of men too in so far as some likeness of such activity belongs to them, none of the other animals is happy, since they in no way share in contemplation. Happiness extends, then, just so far as contemplation does, and those to whom contemplation more fully belongs are more truly happy, not as a mere concomitant but in virtue of the contemplation; for this is in itself precious. Happiness, therefore, must be some form of contemplation."[62]

We believe this, of course, but we would take this further and say that man's perfect happiness consists in the contemplation of the highest being, who is Truth Itself, Goodness Itself, and Beauty Itself, that is, God Himself.

But this tells only half the story. The Jewish understanding of "knowledge" is very different than what we find in the world of the Greek thinkers, and when we consider it in light of the happiness of heaven,

I believe we come to a more complete picture of what the joy of heaven might involve.

For the Jews, to know is to experience, to taste, to enter into a kind of union that is best likened to the relationship between a bride and her groom. At the Annunciation, when the angel revealed to Mary that she will conceive and give birth to a son, she replied: "How can this be since I do not know man" (Lk 1, 34). In other words, Mary had not experienced sexual union with a man, for she was a virgin.

Moreover, to know another is to "convert", that is, to turn to him, to face him, that is, to see him. One turns towards what one loves. Sexual union involves the lover and beloved mutually facing one another. To love the poor, such as the widow and the orphan, is to "see" them, that is, to visit (*visitare, visere*) them.

Jesus pointed out that at the end of time, he will respond to certain others who will claim to have prophesied, exorcised demons, and worked miracles in his name: "I never knew you. Out of my sight, you evildoers!" (Mt 7, 23). In other words, these people did not allow Christ to enter into them, to know them, to visit them, that is, to live in them. "Anyone who loves me will be true to my word, and my Father will love him; we will come to him and make our dwelling place with him" (Jn 14, 23). In the book of Revelation, we read: "Here I stand, knocking at the door. If anyone hears me calling and opens the door, I will enter his house and have supper with him, and he with me" (Rv 3, 20).

To possess truth, that is, to know, is to possess a person, and a bride possesses her husband by receiving him into herself, and he by entering into her. To know is to have entered into a relationship of love. That is why the sexual imagery of the *Song of Songs* is a fitting vehicle to describe more perfectly the relationship between God and Israel: "Let him kiss me with the kisses of his mouth" (Sg 1, 2);[63] "I sleep, but my heart is

189

awake. I hear my Beloved knocking. 'Open to me, my sister, my love, my dove, my perfect one, for my head is covered with dew, my locks with the drops of night. I have taken off my tunic, am I to put it on again? I have washed my feet, am I to dirty them again?' My Beloved thrust his hand through the hole in the door; I trembled to the core of my being" (Sg 5, 2-4).

And so it is true to say that the joy of heaven, because it consists in the possession of God, the possession of the Supreme Good and the Supremely Beautiful, consists at the same time in God, the Supremely Beautiful, turning towards the blessed individually, knowing that person, and delighting in that knowledge: "You ravish my heart, my sister, my promised bride, you ravish my heart with a single one of your glances, with one single pearl of your necklace." (Sg 4, 1-15; Cf. Sg 2, 13-14).

Of course, it is true that God has always known us, for His knowledge is the cause of whatever is. But in heaven we will know that we are known. As St. Paul says: "Then I shall know even as I have been known" (1 Cor 13, 12). Consider the reaction of the young teenager who has just learned that a certain girl has taken a keen interest in him, that she "likes him". He is overjoyed; he is radiant inside; he is given a new lease on life. And when he enters into a relationship with her, he begins to see himself from her point of view.

Similarly, when we "know even as we have been known", we see ourselves in God. In the book of Revelation, we read: "To those who prove victorious I will give the hidden manna and a white stone—a stone with a new name written on it, known only to the man who receives it" (Rev 2, 17). A name is one's identity, and a name given by God, known only to the man who receives it, is indicative of one's profoundest identity. In other words, God will reveal us to ourselves individually, and we will know ourselves in Him, as He knows us, and we will love ourselves perfectly, without any disorder or egoism, and between us will be a knowledge and intimacy, that is, an intimate space in which no one else may enter. Catholic poet Paul Claudel writes:

Then I shall know even as I have been known," says the Apostle. [1 Cor. 13:12] Then shall we see, as unity is seen in variety, the essential rhythm of that movement which is my soul, that measure which is my self. We will not only see it, we will be it, we will present ourselves in the fullness of freedom and knowledge and in the purity of a perfect love. From the bosom of the Lamb we will borrow our individuality, in order to have something to give to Him. In this bitter mortal existence the most poignant joys revealed to our nature are those which attend the creation of a soul by joining of two bodies. Alas, they are but the lowly image of that substantial embrace when the soul, having learned its name and purpose, will surrender itself with a word, will inhale and exhale itself in succession. O continuation of our heart, unutterable word! O dance divine!

All carnal possession is of limited span and duration; what are its transports compared to this royal wedding? "You have made your people feel hardships; you have given us stupefying wine." [Psalm 59:5] What is the seizing of an empire or of a woman's body in a ruthless embrace in comparison with this divine ravishment, like lime seizing sand, and what death (death, our very precious inheritance) grants us in the end so perfect a sacrifice, so generous a restoration, so fatherly and so loving a gift? Such is the reward promised to all the righteous, and this unprecedented wage which amazes the workers of the parable.

But in reality the dowry of each soul will differ from the next, like the will of which it is the embodiment, the purpose that gave it birth, and the one that gave it glory.[64]

191

And so it is true to say that the joy of being in love (*eros*) and having someone in love with you is a distant and faint echo of the intimacy between God and the blessed in heaven.

What would it be like to be completely forgotten, so that no one knows you or your name anymore? Could one conceive of a greater suffering? There is a basic human goodness, an incalculable value that belongs to each person created in the image and likeness of God that demands to be acknowledged, precisely because it is unique, true, good, and beautiful. Joy does not consist only in knowing something other than oneself, but also in being known and loved. In heaven, we will know that we are known, that is, beheld by One to whom no one else can be compared in beauty and goodness, and He will delight in each person's uniqueness, of which He is the cause. And so the joy will be incomparably greater than any kind of experience of being in love with some marvelously beautiful human being.

And so just as the Father loves the Son, and the Son in turn loves the Father, we too will be taken up into an eternal movement of love in which we delight in His happiness and in the perfect praise He receives from the Son, and in which we are delighted and touched that He has turned to us, taken a keen interest in us, and delights in us individually, and we love Him in return, forever.

Some of the greatest wounds that reside deep within a person almost always have to do with broken relationships and unresolved issues with his or her own father, or mother, family or spouse. But the most significant human relationships in our lives, the relationships we have with our father, mother, family, or spouse, and which are all meant to be a prelude to a perfect father's love, a perfect mother's love, the love of a perfect family, and the love of a perfect spouse, will be fully achieved in our union with the one Triune God. In heaven, when we are completely and directly brought into the inner life of the Trinity, we will know the joy of being loved by one who is more perfectly our Father than our own biological father. At the same time, we will know the joy of a perfect Mother's love: the Holy Spirit, the Uncreated Immaculate Conception, who delights eternally in the love between the Father and the Son. That mother's love will know us and take hold of us. At the same time, the joy that we long for of being known, loved, accepted, and embraced by a family, will be perfectly achieved within the inner life of the Trinity, the eternal and perfect family.

Rejoicing in the Happiness of the Blessed

In heaven we delight in the happiness of others, because we love them. We acknowledge their good and delight in it, that is, in their glory and happiness, because their happiness is one with God's; for there is only one happiness in heaven: " ...that they may be one as we are one, Father" (Jn 17, 11). We delight in their glory because they glorify God, and we love them in God; for their glory is a proclamation of His glory, and although they add nothing to His greatness, they glorify Him and so they delight us. What they have become tells of God in some way we do not, and this is what we love. They will proclaim something that I do not, and I will delight in what they say, that they say it, that it belongs to them to say it, and that they are happy to say it. My praise of them, my reverence for them, will be a continuation of my praise and reverence of God. I will totally delight in their happiness, and I will rest in the knowledge that they are at rest, and of course their rest is God's rest in which they share. In heaven, it all begins and ends in God, who is the Alpha and the Omega, the First and the Last (Rev 1, 8). And so our happiness for them is really a function of our happiness for God. He is pleased with them, and so we are pleased with them. That He is pleased with them makes them happy, and so that makes us happy as well—since we love them as much as we love ourselves (as another self). St. Anselm writes about this joy:

> Now surely, if someone else whom you loved in every respect as you do yourself were also to have such happiness, then your own joy would be doubled; for you would rejoice for him no less than for yourself. And if two or three or many more persons were to have such happiness, you would rejoice for each of them as much as for yourself – assuming that you loved each as you do yourself. Therefore, in the case of that perfect love whereby countless happy angels and men shall each love the other no less than himself, each one shall rejoice for every other as much as for himself. So, then, if the heart of man shall scarcely be able to contain its own joy over its own so great good, how shall it be able to contain so many other equally immense joys?
>
> Surely, each person rejoices in another's good fortune to the extent that he loves this other. Therefore, in that perfect happiness, just as each person will love God incomparably more than himself and all those who are with himself, so each will rejoice inestimably more over the happiness of God than over either his own happiness or that of all the others who are with himself. But if with all his heart, all his mind, and all his soul each [of the just] shall so love God that his whole heart, whole mind, and whole soul will not exhaust God's worthiness to be loved, surely with all his heart, all his mind, and all his soul each shall so rejoice that his whole heart, whole mind, and whole soul will not be able to contain the fullness of that joy.[65]

In heaven, there is a desire for the body, but this desire does not compete with the desire for God. The desire for a body is nothing but a function of one's love for God. St. Bernard explains this:

> What of the souls already released from their bodies? We believe that they are overwhelmed in that vast sea of eternal light and of luminous eternity. But no one denies that they still hope and desire to receive their bodies again: whence it is plain that they are not yet wholly transformed, and that something of self remains yet unsurrendered. Not until death is swallowed up in victory, and perennial light overflows the uttermost bounds of darkness, not until celestial glory clothes our bodies, can our souls be freed entirely from self and give themselves up to God. …the spirit would not yearn for reunion with the flesh if without the flesh it could be consummated….The body is a help to the soul that loves God, even when it is ill, even when it is dead, and all the more when it is raised again from the dead: for illness is an aid to penitence; death is the gate of rest; and the resurrection will bring consummation. So, rightly, the soul would not be perfected without the body, since she recognizes that in every condition it has been needful to her good.[66]

There is nothing in heaven the desire of which competes with the desire for God. Whatever we love in heaven, we do so only insofar as it has reference to God, that is, in so far as it is a function of our love for God, or better yet, God's love for Himself. Whatever we see with the glorified body is beheld differently because of our union with God; and that is something we already experience here. Without God, creation becomes nauseatingly empty: "Now I see: I recall better what I felt the other day at the seashore when I held the pebble. It was a sort of sweetish sickness. How unpleasant it was! It came from the stone, I'm sure of it, it passed from the stone to my hand. Yes, that's it, that's just it—

a sort of nausea in the hands".[67] But the more we are immersed in God, the more beautiful creation becomes for us. We see it for what it really is. And so just as "the heavens declare the glory of God; the sky proclaims its builder's craft" (Ps 19, 2), so too in heaven, creation continues to proclaim His glory: "Dew and rain, bless the Lord; praise and exalt him above all forever. Frost and chill, bless the Lord; praise and exalt him above all forever. Ice and snow, bless the Lord; praise and exalt him above all forever...Everything growing from the earth, bless the Lord; praise and exalt him above all forever" (Dn 3, 68-70; 76). These will praise and exalt him above all and forever, eternally, and the blessed in heaven will love them for that reason, in Him in other words; for the blessed, more than ever before, see creation for what it really is, namely a liturgy of praise and thanksgiving. Just as a person in love sees the face of his beloved everywhere, so too wherever one looks and whatever one hears or touches, one perceives what he loves principally, which is God.

Concluding Thoughts

If what is said above is true, it follows that the envious, or the proud, those who love ultimately for the sake of themselves despite appearances to the contrary, will not be able to come to a genuine appreciation of the happiness of the blessed, because they don't know disinterested love, and the happiness of heaven consists in precisely this kind of love. And because it consists in precisely this kind of love, the preparation for heaven is arduous and difficult, because it is ultimately about learning to love, or better yet, learning to lose oneself: "For whoever wishes to save his life will lose it, but whoever loses his life for my sake will find it." (Mt 16, 25)[68]

Love is difficult and requires a great deal of time, tribulation, suffering, as well as prayer and reflection on divine providence. William of St. Thierry writes:

> For through this picturing of your passion, O Christ, our pondering on the good that you have wrought for us leads us forthwith to love the highest good. That good you make us see in the work of salvation, not by an understanding arising from human effort nor by the eyes of our mind that tremble and shrink from your light, but by the peaceful experience of love, and by the good use of our sight and enjoyment of your sweetness, while your wisdom sweetly orders our affairs. ...In sweet meditation on the wonderful sacrament of your passion she muses on the good that you have wrought on our behalf, the good that is as great as you yourself are great, the good that is yourself. She seems to herself to see you face to face when you thus show her, in the cross and in the work of your salvation, the face of the ultimate Good. The cross itself becomes for her the face of a mind that is well-disposed toward God.[69]

The achievement of love requires tribulation and suffering only because inordinate love of self is almost invisible to the one who has it and is far more difficult to uproot—and requires much more time—than the uprooting of a large oak tree, for example.

But now is the only time to begin doing that difficult work: "Behold, now is a very acceptable time; behold, now is the day of salvation" (2 Co 6, 2). Unless a person strives with the utmost effort to enter into the narrow gate of pure disinterested love of God, a gate so small that only a child may enter, one dies unprepared and ill disposed to enjoy the company of the saints, who will inevitably appear as a company of strangers.

Index

Notes

[1] *On Being and Essence*, Prologue.

[2] Angels are not eternal. Only God, who is pure Act of Being, is eternal. But the duration proper to pure spirits is traditionally referred to as eviternity. "Each time for example that an angel turns his thought toward a new object, he marks so to speak the indivisible aevum, in which he remains forever, of the initial point and of the final point of an operation which, in the immobility of an instance which endures, coincides with a certain flow of our time". Jacques Maritain. *On The Church of Christ*, Notre Dame, University of Notre Dame Press, 1973, p. 47. In short, the angelic intellect does not depend upon data from the senses, as does the human intellect. As Aristotle pointed out: "Nothing is in the intellect that is not first in the senses." The angelic mind is unencumbered by matter.

[3] St. Gregory the Great, Pseudo-Dionysius, and St. Thomas Aquinas all speak of the hierarchies of angels. Aquinas points out that it is inevitable that the multitude of angels should form a hierarchy; for each angel is its own species. This is true because an angel has no matter, and matter is one of the principles of individuation. It is quantified matter that enables a form to exist in a multiplicity of instances, just as the one form of a cookie cutter can be multiplied into many instances as long as one has enough dough, which is the matter of the cookie. But if an angel has no matter, that which distinguishes one angel from another is located in the form. Hence, one angel is formally (specifically) different from another, as one number is formally different from another number; for just as one number is either higher or lower than another number, so too is one angel either higher or lower than another angel. All human beings are equal because all humans have the same nature, and each one is different not by virtue of our form, but on the basis of our matter.

Tradition speaks of three hierarchies of angels, each composed of three "choirs." The highest angels are the Seraphim. The name "seraphim" means "carriers of fire." Scripture speaks of God as a "consuming fire" (Heb 12, 29). Fire is a symbol of the divine love. If one gets too close to a fire, one will inevitably catch fire. The seraphim are so close to God that they are "on fire" with the divine love. Pseudo-Dionysius writes: "For the designation seraphim really teaches this--a perennial circling around the divine things, penetrating warmth, the overflowing heat of a movement which never falters and never fails, a capacity to stamp their own image on subordinates by arousing and uplifting in them too a like flame, the same warmth. It means also the power to purify by means of the lightning flash and the flame. It means the ability to hold unveiled and undiminished both the light they have and the illumination they give out. It means the capacity to push aside and to do away with every obscuring shadow." *The Celestial Hierarchy* 7, 1, in *Pseudo-Dionysius: The Complete Works*. Translated by Colm Luibheid. New York: Paulist Press, 1987.

The word "cherubim" means "fullness of knowledge". These highly intelligent creatures are below the seraphim because love is greater than knowledge. "The name cherubim signifies the power to know and to see God, to receive the greatest gifts of his light, to contemplate the divine splendor in primordial power, to be filled with the gifts that bring wisdom and to share these generously with subordinates as a part of the beneficent outpouring of wisdom." *Loc. cit.*

The angels of the third choir on the first hierarchy are called the thrones. They are characterized by their super eminent humility. Dionysius writes: The title of the most sublime and exalted thrones conveys that in them there is a transcendence over every earthly defect, as shown by their upward-bearing toward the ultimate heights, that they are forever separated from what is inferior, that they are completely intent upon remaining always and forever in the presence of him who is truly the most high, that, free of all passion and material concern, they are utterly available to receive the divine visitation, that they bear God and are ever open, like servants, to welcome God. *loc. cit.*

The middle hierarchy is made up of the Dominations, Celestial Virtues, and Powers. The angles of the first hierarchy enlighten all the angels of this second hierarchy. They "pour out" all they have received from God, thereby elevating them as much as they are able. The lowest hierarchy are composed of the Principalities (guardians of nations), archangels (guardians of leaders of state, bishops, and important personages), and angels (guardians of ordinary people). These angels are elevated by the outpourings of the angels of the second hierarchy. The angels on the lowest hierarchy are intimately involved in human affairs, even thought we are largely unaware of it. It is in this way that they share in the sheer generosity of divine providence, as God's gifts go largely unacknowledged, so too the activity of the angels among us.

[4] *Dictionary of Biblical Theology*: New Revised Edition. New York: Seabury Press, 1973. s.v. "Satan".

[5] Note how the miracles of Christ begin with his spoken word: "He woke up, rebuked the wind, and said to the sea, "Quiet! Be still!"; "He took the child by the hand and said to her, "Talitha Koum,", which means, "Little girl, I say to you, arise!"; "When it was evening, they brought him many who were possessed by demons, and he drove out the spirits by a word and cured all the sick, to fulfill what had been said by Isaiah the prophet." The divine nature speaks real being into existence. This is not possible for any creature whose essence is distinct from its existence. Jesus' human nature does not have an act of existing (*esse*) that is distinct from his divine nature. Jesus is one Person, not two. And so creation can only obey the voice of Christ;

204

for he is the Word through whom all things came to be. The very existence of things depends entirely on this Word.

[6] The sacrifice of the cross is the visible and historical expression of the Son's love for the Father, a visible expression of the inner life of the Triune God. The Father and the Son, as was pointed out, are really distinct (not separate). The Father knows Himself through His word (Son), for the Son is the perfect image of the Father. Recall that all the perfections attributed to God are identical to His existence. For example, God does not have justice, love, or beauty. Rather, God is His Justice. He is Essentially Good and Beautiful, and God is His Love. For there is no composition in God--otherwise God would be related to these added perfections as potency is related to act. But God is pure Act of Being. Similarly, the Word by which the Father knows Himself is identical to His Existence. Hence, Father and Son are one nature. Now, the Father loves what He knows, namely the Son. The Son in turn loves the Father. The love by which the Father loves the Son, and the love by which the Son loves the Father, is also identical to the divine nature. Hence, the mutual love of the Father and the Son is infinite, divine, and thus personal. It is a love that is a distinct Person of the Trinity, the Third Person of the Trinity, namely, the Holy Spirit.

[7] *Apology I*, chapter 66.

[8] *Trac. in Io*. VIII.

[9] *Ibid., VIII.*

[10] *Epistle to the Smyrnaeans*.

[11] *Against Heresies*, bk I, 10.

[12] *Ibid., bk III, 3.*

[13] "Clerical and Consecrated Life and Service", *The Way of the Lord Jesus*, Vol 4, Unpublished Text. p. 20.

[14] "It is extremely convenient to have a label for the political and economic viewpoint elaborated in this book. The rightful and proper label is liberalism. Unfortunately, "As a supreme, if unintended compliment, the enemies of the system of private enterprise have thought it wise to

appropriate its label" (Joseph Schumpeter, *History of Economic Analysis* (New York: Oxford University Press, 1954) p. 394), so that liberalism has, in the United States, come to have a very different meaning than it did in the nineteenth century or does today over much of the Continent of Europe.

As it developed in the late eighteenth and early nineteenth centuries, the intellectual movement that went under the name of liberalism emphasized freedom as the ultimate goal and the individual as the ultimate entity in the society. It supported laissez faire at home as a means of reducing the role of the state in economic affairs and thereby enlarging the role of the individual; it supported free trade abroad as a means of linking the nations of the world together peacefully and democratically. In political matters, it supported the development of representative government and of parliamentary institutions, reduction in the arbitrary power of the state, and protection of the civil freedoms of individuals.

Beginning in the late nineteenth century, and especially after 1930 in the United States, the term liberalism came to be associated with a very different emphasis, particularly in economic policy. It came to be associated with a readiness to rely primarily on the state rather than on private voluntary arrangements to achieve objectives regarded as desirable. The catchwords became welfare and equality rather than freedom. The nineteenth-century liberal regarded an extension of freedom as the most effective way to promote welfare and equality; the twentieth-century liberal regards welfare and equality as either prerequisites of or alternatives to freedom. In the name of welfare and equality, the twentieth-century liberal has come to favor a revival of the very policies of state intervention and paternalism against which classical liberalism fought. In the very act of turning the clock back to seventeenth-century mercantilism, he is fond of castigating true liberals as reactionary!

The change in the meaning attached to the term liberalism is more striking in economic matters than in political. The twentieth-century liberal, like the nineteenth-century liberal, favors parliamentary institutions, representative government, civil rights, and so on. Yet even in political matters, there is a notable difference. Jealous of liberty, and hence fearful of centralized power, whether in governmental or private hands, the nineteenth-century liberal favored political decentralization. Committed to action and confident of the beneficence of power so long as it is in the hands of a government ostensibly controlled by the electorate, the twentieth-century liberal favors centralized government. He will resolve any doubt about where power should be located in favor of the state instead of the city, of the federal government instead of the state, and of a world organization instead of a national government.

Because of the corruption of the term liberalism, the views that formerly went under that name are now often labeled conservatism. But this is not a satisfactory alternative. The nineteenth-century liberal was a radical, both in the etymological sense of going to the root of the matter, and in the political sense of favoring major changes in social institutions. So too must be his modern heir. We do not wish to conserve the state interventions that have interfered so greatly with our freedom, though, of course, we do wish to conserve those that have promoted it. Moreover, in practice, the term conservatism has come to cover so wide a range of views, and views so incompatible with one another, that we shall no doubt see the growth of hyphenated designations, such as libertarian-conservative and aristocratic-conservative." Milton Friedman. *Capitalism and Freedom*. Chicago: University of Chicago Press, 1962. Introduction.

[15] V. I. Lenin, "The Tasks of the Youth Leagues," Speech delivered at the Third All Russian Young Communist League, October 2, 1920, in Lenin, *Selected Works*, London:

Lawrence & Wishart, 1947, Vol. II, pp. 669, 670. Quoted in Jacques Maritain. *Moral Philosophy*. New York: Charles Scribner's Sons, 1964, p. 250.

[16] See *Ibid.*, pp. 253-256.

[17] *Quadragesimo Anno*, 132.

[18] *Octagesimo Adveniens*, 31.

[19] Quoted in Katherine Burton, *Leo the Thirteenth: The First Modern Pope*. New York: David McKay Co., 1962, p. 171.

[20] "How an incredibly complex, high-tech economy can operate without any central direction is baffling to many. The last President of the Soviet Union, Mikhail Gorbachev, is said to have asked British Prime Minister Margaret Thatcher: How do you see to it that people get food? The answer was that she didn't. Prices did that. Moreover, the British people were better fed than people in the Soviet Union, even though the British have not produced enough food to feed themselves in more than a century. Prices bring them food from other countries.

Without the role of prices, imagine what a monumental bureaucracy it would take to see to it that the city of London alone is supplied with the tons of food, of every variety, which it consumes every day. Yet such an army of bureaucrats can be dispensed with—and the people that would be needed in such a bureaucracy can do productive work elsewhere in the economy—because the simple mechanism of prices does the same job faster, cheaper, and better." Thomas Sowell, *Basic Economics*. New York: Basic Books, 2011, p. 12.

[21] Thomas Sowell outlines these two visions and draws out their fundamental characteristics as they pertain to law and economics in particular. The one he refers to as the constrained vision of man (which would correspond to the first view I framed above), the other as the unconstrained vision of man (corresponding to the latter view I framed above). He writes: "Both constrained and unconstrained visions are ultimately concerned with social results. The

208

unconstrained vision seeks directly to achieve those results socially—that is, through collective decisions prescribing the desired outcomes. The constrained vision considers it beyond the capability of any manageable set of decision-makers to marshal the requisite knowledge, and dangerous to concentrate sufficient power, to carry out their decisions, even if it were possible.

Given the unconstrained vision, which permits results to be directly prescribed, its basic concepts are expressed in terms of results. The degree of freedom is thus the degree to which one's desires can be realized, without regard to whether the obstacles to full realization be the deliberately imposed restrictions of government or the lack of circumstantial prerequisites. Justice is likewise a question of outcomes, and the justice or injustice of a society can therefore be determined directly by those outcomes, whether they be the result of conscious decisions, social attitudes, or circumstances inherited from the past. Power is likewise defined by results: If **A** can cause **B** to do what **A** wants done, then **A** has power over **B**, regardless of whether **A**'s inducements to **B** are positive (rewards) or negative (penalties). Equality too is a result, the degree of equality or inequality being a directly observable fact."

Further on in the chapter "Summary and Conclusions", he writes: "The two visions differ not only in how they see differences between themselves but also in how they see differences between ordinary individuals and those more intellectually or morally advanced. In the unconstrained vision, where the intellectual and moral potential of man vastly exceeds the levels currently observable in the general population, there is more room for individual variation in intellectual and moral performance than in the constrained vision, where the elite and the masses are both penned within relatively narrow limits. Striking moral and intellectual differences are recognized by those with the constrained vision, but are regarded as either too exceptional to form the basis of social policy or as confined to a small area out of a vast spectrum of human concerns. Given the inherent limitations of human beings, the extraordinary person (morally or intellectually) is extraordinary only within some very limited area, perhaps at the cost of grave deficiencies elsewhere, and may well have blind spots which prevent him from seeing some things which are clearly visible to ordinary people.

Differences between the moral-intellectual elite and the masses are crucial, especially to modern conflicts of visions over the degree of surrogate decision-making, whether by politicians, judges, or various agencies and commissions. Both visions try to make the locus of discretion coincide with the locus of knowledge, but they conceive of knowledge in such radically different terms as to lead to opposite conclusions as to where discretion should be vested.

To those with the unconstrained vision, who see knowledge and reason as concentrated in those who have advanced furthest toward the ultimate potential of man, surrogate decision-making—economic "planning," judicial activism, etc.—is essential. These surrogate decision-makers must attempt both to influence beforehand and to revise afterward the decisions made by those less accomplished in intellectual or moral terms. But to those with the constrained vision, each individual's knowledge is so grossly inadequate, compared to the knowledge mobilized systemically through economic markets, traditional values, and other social processes, that surrogate decision-makers in general—and non-elected judges in particular—should severely limit themselves to drawing up rules defining the boundaries of others' discretion, not second-guess the decisions actually made within those boundaries. In the constrained vision, the loci of discretion should be as widely scattered as possible, the inevitable errors resulting being accepted as a trade-off, no solution being possible. Thomas Sowell (2007). *A Conflict of Visions: Ideological Origins of Political Struggles* [Kobo version]. Retrieved from Kobo.com. See Summary and Conclusions. Published by Basic Books, New York.

[22] *Quadragesimo Anno,* 79.

[23] *Centesimus Annus,* 48.3-4.

[24] "Socrates' Defense (Apology)", translated by Hugh Tredennick. *The Collected Dialogues of Plato*. New Jersey: Princeton University Press, 1961. Pp 7-8.

[25] St. Thomas writes: "It is impossible to attain to the knowledge of the Trinity by natural reason. For, as above explained (12, 4, 12), man cannot obtain the knowledge of God by natural reason except from creatures. Now creatures lead us to the knowledge of God, as effects do to their cause. Accordingly, by natural reason we can know of God that only which of necessity belongs to Him as the principle of things, and we have cited this fundamental principle in treating of God as above (12, 12). Now, the creative power of God is common to the whole Trinity; and hence it belongs to the unity of the essence, and not to the distinction of the persons. Therefore, by natural reason we can know what belongs to the unity of the essence, but not what belongs to the distinction of the persons." *S.T.*, I. Q. 32. a. 1.

[26] A thing is knowable insofar as it is in act. For example, pure potentiality is unknowable in itself; one cannot know that which is not actually anything. A material thing, because it is a unity of potency and act (matter and form), is not entirely transparent to the human intellect. The active mind must abstract the essence from the individuating conditions surrounding the phantasm to render the thing actually intelligible. Nevertheless, the essence of a material thing includes matter, which is why even when apprehended by the mind, we still do not fully know the essences of material things, which is evident in our imperfect definitions. There remains an opacity that is the result of the potentiality of matter.

[27] St. Thomas writes: "Intelligent substances, the noblest of creatures, express themselves through knowledge and love. Thus they bear the image of the uncreated Trinity. Their own thoughts and their loves, however, are not persons; their understanding and affections are not their substance, but qualities about them. Only with God is understanding and loving his very self, only with him are his Word and Love persons." *Disputations*, X, *de Potentia,* I.

[28] See Larry Azar. *Man: Computer, Ape, or Angel*. Massachusetts: The Christopher Publishing House, 1989. pp. 185-186.

[29] "It may be said that God has a rational "nature," if reason be taken to mean, not discursive thought, but in a general sense, an intelligent nature. But God cannot be called an "individual" in the sense that His individuality comes from matter; but only in the sense which implies incommunicability. "Substance" can be applied to God in the sense of signifying self-subsistence. There are some, however, who say that the definition of Boethius, quoted above (1), is not a definition of person in the sense we use when speaking of persons in God. Therefore Richard of St. Victor amends this definition by adding that "Person" in God is "the incommunicable existence of the divine nature."" *S.T.*, I, Q. 29. 3, ad 4.

[30] "That which proceeds by way of intelligence, as word, proceeds according to similitude, as also that which proceeds by way of nature; thus, as above explained (27, 3), the procession of the divine Word is the very same as generation by way of nature. But love, as such, does not proceed as the similitude of that whence it proceeds; although in God love is co-essential as being divine; and therefore the procession of love is not called generation in God." *S.T.*, I. Q. 30. 1, ad 2.

[31] "For as when a thing is understood by anyone, there results in the one who understands a conception of the object understood, which conception we call word; so

212

when anyone loves an object, a certain impression results, so to speak, of the thing loved in the affection of the lover; by reason of which the object loved is said to be in the lover; as also the thing understood is in the one who understands; so that when anyone understands and loves himself he is in himself, not only by real identity, but also as the object understood is in the one who understands, and the thing loved is in the lover. As regards the intellect, however, words have been found to describe the mutual relation of the one who understands the object understood, as appears in the word "to understand"; and other words are used to express the procession of the intellectual conception—namely, "to speak," and "word." Hence in God, "to understand" is applied only to the essence; because it does not import relation to the Word that proceeds; whereas "Word" is said personally, because it signifies what proceeds; and the term "to speak" is a notional term as importing the relation of the principle of the Word to the Word Himself. On the other hand, on the part of the will, with the exception of the words "dilection" and "love," which express the relation of the lover to the object loved, there are no other terms in use, which express the relation of the impression or affection of the object loved, produced in the lover by fact that he loves— to the principle of that impression, or "vice versa." And therefore, on account of the poverty of our vocabulary, we express these relations by the words "love" and "dilection": just as if we were to call the Word "intelligence conceived," or "wisdom begotten."" *S.T.*, I. Q. 37. 1.

[32] "The procession of the Word is called generation in the proper sense of the term, whereby it is applied to living things. Now the relation of the principle of generation in perfect living beings is called paternity; and the relation of the one proceeding from the principle is called filiation. But the procession of Love has no proper name of its own (27, 4); and so neither have the ensuing relations a proper name of their own. The relation of the principle of this

procession is called spiration; and the relation of the person proceeding is called procession: although these two names belong to the processions or origins themselves, and not to the relations." *S.T.,* I. Q. 28. 4.

[33] Russian Philosopher Vladimir Solovyov writes: "The meaning of human love, speaking generally, is the justification and salvation of individuality through the sacrifice of egoism. The falsehood and evil of egoism by no means consist in the fact that the egoist values himself too highly, credits himself with absolute significance and infinite worth. In this he is correct, because every human subject, as an independent center of living powers, as a potentiality of infinite perfection, as a being capable in consciousness and in his life of accommodating absolute truth--every person, as such, possesses absolute significance and worth. In every human being there is something absolutely irreplaceable, and one cannot value oneself too highly. (In the words of the gospel: "What shall a man give in exchange for his soul?) Failure to recognize one's own absolute significance is equivalent to a denial of human worth; this is a basic error and the origin of all unbelief. If one is so faint-hearted that he is powerless even to believe in himself, how can he believe in anything else? The basic falsehood and evil of egoism lie not in this absolute self-consciousness and self-evaluation of the subject, but in the fact that, ascribing to himself in all justice an absolute significance, he unjustly refuses to others this same significance. Recognizing himself as a center of life (which as a matter of fact he is), he relegates others to the circumference of his own being and leaves them only an external and relative value." *The Meaning of Love*. London, Floris Books. pp. 42-44.

[34] St. Thomas writes: "Although the angels and the souls of the saints are always with God, nevertheless, if plurality of persons did not exist in God, He would be alone or solitary. For solitude is not removed by association with anything that is extraneous in nature; thus anyone is said

to be alone in a garden, though many plants and animals are with him in the garden. Likewise, God would be alone or solitary, though angels and men were with Him, supposing that several persons were not within Him. Therefore the society of angels and of souls does not take away absolute solitude from God; much less does it remove respective solitude, in reference to a predicate."
S.T., I. Q. 31. 3. ad 1.

[35] Richard of St. Victor. *Book Three of the Trinity*. Ch. XI. Translated by Grover Zinn. New York: Paulist Press.

[36] *Loc.cit.*

[37] *The Beatitudes*, Sermon 1, in *Ancient Christian Writers: The Lord's Prayer, The Beatitudes*. New York: Newman Press. 1954.

[38] *A Great and Glorious Game*. New York: Algonquin Books, 1997, p. 111.

[39] *Ibid.*, pp.12-13.

[40] He moves the will of man, and in doing so, makes it possible for man to choose freely. No finite creature can move something without determining it. If I move a garbage can, I determine the new place it will occupy. But God is not a finite creature limited in power. He can move the will of man without determining it. God moves the will of man towards the good in general, that is, the good without qualification.

Now the will of man needs to be moved by God, because nothing moves itself from potency to actuality except by something already in act. Man cannot move his own will from the state of potentially willing to actually willing, for a thing cannot give to itself a perfection that it does not have. And no other creature can move the will, for the will is an immaterial power. Moreover, the very idea of something outside the will moving it is contradictory; such an act of the will would be an act of my will without being my act of the will, which is absurd. Only God can and must move the will, and He alone moves it without determining it. It is man who determines himself to this or that option.

Free-choice is the ability to deliberate on various options each containing limited goods. To choose is to cut off deliberation, or to decide on a specific course of action. In doing so, man determines himself in relation to these limited goods, and in so doing he determines the kind of person that he is. But he cannot do so without his will being first moved by God, just as man cannot actually turn the car to the left or the right unless the car is moving.

[41] J. P. de Caussade. *Self-Abandonment to Divine Providence*. Rockford, Tan Books, 1987. p. 28.

[42] *Ibid.*, p. 104.

[43] *Ibid.*, p. 81

[44] *The Business of Heaven*, Glasgow, Harper Collins, 1984. p. 121.

[45] *A Portrait of the Artist as a Young Man*. New York: Penguin Books, 1976, p. 131-132.

[46] *Ibid.*, p. 122.

[47] *Story of a Soul*, ch. 9

[48] Bernard Nathanson. "Confessions of an Ex-Abortionist" *(1997). Catholic Educator's Resource Center.* http://www.catholiceducation.org/articles/abortion/ab0005.html.

[49] *Ibid.*

[50] St. Thomas Aquinas points out that every human being has a natural knowledge of God, albeit confused and general. For it is not possible to desire what one does not know, and all human persons desire happiness, one that is final, complete, sufficient unto itself, and enduring. But only God answers to these properties, for He alone is final, complete, sufficient unto Himself, and eternal. He writes: "To know that God exists in a general and confused way is implanted in us by nature, inasmuch as God is man's beatitude. For man naturally desires happiness, and what is naturally desired by man must be naturally known to him. This, however, is not to know absolutely that God exists;

just as to know that someone is approaching is not the same as to know that Peter is approaching, even though it is Peter who is approaching; for many there are who imagine that man's perfect good which is happiness, consists in riches, and others in pleasures, and others in something else." *S. T.,* I, q. 2, 1, ad 1.

[51] St. Bernard of Clairvaux, *On Loving God*, ch. 5.

[52] *Sermons of St. Alphonsus Liguori*, Serm. 16, 4. Second Sunday of Lent. Illinois, Tan Books, 1982.

[53] Joseph Owens writes: "...for Aquinas, a thing can have three ways of existing. Its first and most fundamental way of existence is in the divine intellect. There it is the same in reality as the divine essence, differing only in concept. The second way is by existing in itself, or in an angelic mind. Both these types of existence depend immediately upon the first type. The third way of existing is in the human intellect, and is based immediately upon the existence of the things in themselves. The existence of things in the divine intellect is accordingly for Aquinas a much stronger and more perfect existence than their existence in themselves. It is prior to the real existence in the created world, and not dependent on it. It is an existence that lasts forever, because it is really identical with the creative essence. This eternal existence of things may be found instinctively surmised at times. On the death of a family pet dog known from their earliest conscious years, children will react with the spontaneous conviction that some day they will be with Heidi again. Browning was able to write in his poem "Abt Vogler": "There never shall be one lost good; what was, shall be as before." Both the instinctive reaction and the poetic inspiration seem well grounded in reality when they are assessed from the viewpoints of Aquinas' metaphysics. In its highest point of elevation the existence of every creature is eternal. ...all things whatsoever have eternal existence in the divine creative intellect, and that this is the highest type of existence they can have.

All things, it will mean, are possessed in the beatific vision of the divine creative essence. They are possessed cognitionally in it in their highest kind of existence. Anything missed or sacrificed for the sake of the right or the holy is accordingly never lost. Rather, eternal possession of it is assured. "Possession," in fact, may be a weak word here. The "possession" consists in being those things cognitionally, and not in the comparatively weak way of a cognition that follows upon and is dependent upon the things in their sensible existence. Rather, it is like the angelic cognition in having them as objects in their highest way of being. In the gradated orders of existence listed by Aquinas the existence of things in the divine intellect is prior to their existence in themselves, while their existence in themselves is prior to their existence in present human cognition. It is not hard to see in this perspective the definitive answer to the objection that contemplation is a shadowy and unreal possession of things, like having them in a day dream. On the contrary, just as existence for sensible things in themselves is real in comparison with their cognitional existence in the human mind at present, so their existence in the beatific cognition is of a higher type than their real existence just in themselves. It is in this sense that "every perfection of things good" is attained in the beatific contemplation, when explained in the metaphysical perspective of Aquinas." *Human Destiny: Some Problems for Catholic Philosophy*. The Catholic University of America Press, 1985. p. 45-46.

[54] "How great is the sweetness which a soul experiences when, in the time of prayer, God, by a ray of his own light, shows to her his goodness and his mercies towards her, and particularly the love which Jesus Christ has borne to her in his passion! She feels her heart melting and as it were dissolved through love. But in this life we do not see God as he really is: we see him as it were in the dark". St. Alphonsus Liguori, op.cit., 16, 6.

[55] *Ibid.*, 16, 8. In the same sermon, he writes: "They shall be inebriated with the plenty of thy house" – Ps., xxxv. 9. In beholding the beauty of God, the soul shall be so inflamed and so inebriated with divine love, that she shall remain happily lost in God; for she shall entirely forget herself, and for all eternity shall think only of loving and praising the immense good which she shall possess for ever, without the fear of having it in her power ever to lose it. 16, 8.

[56] St. Bernard of Clairvaux. *On Loving God*, ch. 11.

[57] Quoted in *On Prayer: Spiritual Instructions on the Various States of Prayer According to the Doctrine of Bossuet Bishop of Meaux 1931.* London: Burns and Oates & Washbourne, 1931. p. 90. He also writes: "It is said that Christians have become accustomed to seek God only for their interest and beatitude: but who has accustomed them? Not the Bishop of Meaux, who set himself to show from the Scriptures, from the holy doctors and most of all from S. Augustine, that the love which we bear to God as a beatifying object (that is, as the source of our happiness), necessarily presupposes the love we have for him because of his perfections and his infinite lovableness, without which charity itself would no longer exist, bereft of its principal object, which is the excellence of the divine nature." *Ibid.*, p. 90-91.

[58] *On Loving God*, ch. 9.

[59] St. Bernard also writes: "How blessed is he who reaches the fourth degree of love, wherein one loves himself only in God! ...In Him should all our affections center, so that in all things we should seek only to do His will, not to please ourselves. And real happiness will come, not in gratifying our desires or in gaining transient pleasures, but in accomplishing God's will for us....To reach this state is to become godlike. As a drop of water poured into wine loses itself, and takes the color and savor of wine; or as a bar of iron, heated red-hot, becomes like fire itself, forgetting its own nature; or as the air, radiant with sun-

beams, seems not so much to be illuminated as to be light itself; so in the saints all human affections melt away by some unspeakable transmutation into the will of God. For how could God be all in all, if anything merely human remained in man? The substance will endure, but in another beauty, a higher power, a greater glory." *Ibid.*, ch. 10.

[60] The distance between the creature and God is an infinite distance, and so nothing but the Divine Nature Itself, which is infinite, can bridge that infinite distance.

[61] St. Francis de Sales writes: "the height of love's ecstasy is to have our will not in its own contentment but in God's". *Treatise on the Love of God.* Translated by Rev. Henry Benedict Mackey, O.S.B. Illinois: Tan Books, 1997. Bk 6, ch. 2.

[62] Bk 10, 8: "...the activity of our intelligence constitutes the complete happiness of man,...So if it is true that intelligence is divine in comparison with man, then a life guided by intelligence is divine in comparison with human life. We must not follow those who advise us to have human thoughts, since we are only men, and mortal thoughts, as mortals should; on the contrary, we should try to become immortal as far as that is possible and do our utmost to live in accordance with what is highest in us." *EN,* 10, 7

[63] St. Francis de Sales writes: "The great Solomon describes, in an admirably delicious manner, the loves of the Saviour and the devout soul, in that divine work which for its excellent sweetness is named the Canticle of Canticles....Now making the spouse or bride begin first by manner of a certain surprise of love, he first puts into her mouth this ejaculation: Let him kiss me with the kiss of his mouth. Notice, Theotimus, how the soul, in the person of this shepherdess, has but the one aim, in the first expression of her desire, of a chaste union with her spouse, protesting that it is the only end of her ambition and the only thing she aspires after; for, I pray you, what other

thing would this first sigh intimate?...A kiss from all ages as by natural instinct has been employed to represent perfect love, that is, the union of hearts, and not without cause: we express and make known our passions and the movements which our souls have in common with the animals, by our eyes, eyebrows, forehead and the rest of our countenance....And thus one mouth is applied to another in kissing to testify that we would desire to pour out one soul into the other, to unite them reciprocally in a perfect union." *Treatise on the Love of God*, Bk 1, ch. 9.

[64] *I Believe in God: A Meditation on the Apostle's Creed*. ed. Agnes Du Sarment. Trans. Helen Weaver. New York:. Holt, Rinehart and Winston, 1963. p 298-299. Claudel writes: "Such is this new name mentioned in the Bible, this proper name by which we have been called unto eternal life, this unutterable name which always remains a secret between the Creator and us, and which is imparted to no other. To learn this name is to understand our own nature, to be sustained by our own raison d'etre. Like a word made up of vowels and consonants, our soul draws from God with each breath the fullness of its resonance. Thus, for the soul, birth will be identical with understanding, with a fully illuminated awareness". *Ibid.*, p. 309.

[65] *Proslogion*, ch. 25. In the same chapter, he writes: "Do you delight in friendship? They shall love God more than themselves and shall love one another as themselves; and God shall love them more than they love themselves. For through Him they shall love Him and themselves and one another; but He loves Himself and them through Himself. Do you want unison? They shall all have one will, because they shall have no will except the will of God. Do you desire power? They shall be all-powerful in will, even as God is all-powerful in will. For as God is able to do through Himself that which He wills, so they shall be able to do through Him that which they shall will. For as they shall will nothing other than He shall will, so He shall will whatever they shall will. And what He shall will must come

to pass. Do honor and riches delight you? God shall set His good and faithful servants over many things; indeed, they shall be, as well as be called, sons of God and gods. And where His Son shall be, there they too shall be, for they are heirs of God and joint-heirs with Christ. Do you want true security? Surely they shall be certain that they shall never in any way lack these many goods – or rather this one Good – even as they shall be certain (1) that they shall not lose it of their own free wills, (2) that God, who loves them, shall not rend it away from them against their wills while they are loving Him, and (3) that nothing more powerful than God shall separate them from God against their wills. But where goodness of such quality and of such enormity is present, how rich and how extensive must be the corresponding joy! O human heart, heart beset with need, heart versed in tribulation – yea, overwhelmed with tribulation – how much you would rejoice were you to abound in all these goods!" *Anselm of Canterbury*, Volume One, edited and translated by Jasper Hopkins and Herbert W. Richardson. Toronto, Edwin Mellen Press, 1974.

[66] *On Loving God*, ch. 11.

[67] *Nausea*, translated by Lloyd Alexander. New York: New Directions, 1964, p. 10-11.

[68] "I know your longings and I have heard your frequent sighs. Already you wish to be in the liberty of the glory of the sons of God. Already you desire the delights of the eternal home, the heavenly land that is full of joy. But that hour is not yet come. There remains yet another hour, a time of war, of labor, and of trial. You long to be filled with the highest good, but you cannot attain it now. I am that sovereign Good. Await Me, until the kingdom of God shall come.

You must still be tried on earth, and exercised in many things. Consolation will sometimes be given you, but the complete fullness of it is not granted. Take courage, therefore, and be strong both to do and to suffer what is contrary to nature.

You must put on the new man. You must be changed into another man. You must often do the things you do not wish to do and forego those you do wish. What pleases others will succeed; what pleases you will not. The words of others will be heard; what you say will be accounted as nothing. Others will ask and receive; you will ask and not receive. Others will gain great fame among men; about you nothing will be said. To others the doing of this or that will be entrusted; you will be judged useless. At all this nature will sometimes be sad, and it will be a great thing if you bear this sadness in silence. For in these and many similar ways the faithful servant of the Lord is wont to be tried, to see how far he can deny himself and break himself in all things....

Bow humbly, therefore, under the will of all, and do not heed who said this or commanded that. But let it be your special care when something is commanded, or even hinted at, whether by a superior or an inferior or an equal, that you take it in good part and try honestly to perform it. Let one person seek one thing and another something else. Let one glory in this, another in that, and both be praised a thousand times over. But as for you, rejoice neither in one or the other, but only in contempt of yourself and in My pleasure and honor. Let this be your wish: That whether in life or in death God may be glorified in you." Thomas a Kempis. *The Imitation of Christ*, Bk 3, ch. 49.

[69] William of St. Thierry, *The Works of William of St Thierry*, Volume 1: *On Contemplating God, Prayer, Meditations.* Trans. Sister Penelope, CSMV. Michigan: Cistercian Publications, 1979. Meditation 10:7, p. 153-154.

223

Made in the USA
Lexington, KY
21 June 2013